THE BARE MELCESSITIES

Outskirts Press, Inc.
Denver, Colorado

THE BARE MELCESSITIES

MELANIE LUTZ

Pete : Kim
You were there in the
beginning. You were
there through it all. .
Thanks for your advice, friendship
Love & support.
  Lots of love,   oxox
      Melanie

To Heather Rem and Vanessa Bland
and all my purposeful powerful sister friends whose
laughs, loves and lives beat into a wondrous future
filled with limitless possibilities.

TABLE OF CONTENTS

Prelude

Throughout our lives we yearn to know ourselves and who we really are in our lifetimes.

What matters most to us. What makes us tick.

Some of us find this knowing only in the last days of our lives. Others when overwhelmed by illness. For me, it came in the form of musical theater and a year living through a breakup and divorce.

My whole life I've loved musicals. All forms. The beginnings of my obsession started with Sunday night childhood pajama viewings of The Wonderful World Of Disney. No matter what was going on, the images and music and morals and metaphors danced across the screen bringing wonder and joy and delight.

It isn't an accident when I was struggling with separation, divorce, depression and a long battle with high-achieving, low self esteem, that some part of my brain would connect with my passion and pull a song from the Disney cannon to guide me through. It floated into my head, "look for the bare necessities" find a different way. The notion wouldn't go away. It kept haunting me. Let go of all the things that don't make you come alive; give up on some long-knitted dream that wasn't working, and begin again. The Bare Necessities. The Bare Necessities. Hmmmm. It kept playing in my mind like a mantra. What would it mean if I let everything go and just focused on the basics? Baring down, bare down, it couldn't be more on point. I needed to strip everything away and bare my truth. I needed to throw over the current Mel regime, to understand the essentials, and build that essence into a new me. I knew I could be free of my struggles. I knew I could be.

The Bare Melcessities was born.

There are a lot of goofy realities that constitute living in the two thousands. Technology, isolation, community, colossal and constant information creating an ever growing disconnect. I'm sharing a little bit of my own coming to some type of knowing. My own version of baring it all. A series of feelings, thoughts and perhaps a revelation or two presented in a written self portrait. At worst it will help me. At best my hopes are that you will join me on a journey of exploration, become witnesses to the truths that surround all of us and get bare.

The idea of a self portrait containing ideas, thoughts, poems, lyrics, and moments of memory flashing in and out of a year spent starting over, seemed like the best gift I could give myself. What better way to celebrate a year where I finally grew up and into myself. It is the ultimate kaleidoscope of what can make and unmake a life or better yet, unmake and make a life.

"Bit by bit putting it together. Every moment makes a contribution, every little detail plays a part." Stephen Sondheim's luminating song from Sunday in the Park with George gets me thinking that everything, the moments, the choices, the happenstance, the occurrences, all build toward a work of art that is the life in which we live.

These pieces complete a picture. Me. Starting over. Inch by inch. Mile by mile. Day by day. Breath by breath.

Nothing more. Nothing less.

The Great Tiny Closet
Flood of '08

Sometimes it is the simplest sayings that become the most profound.

Topping the list.

Home is where the heart is.

Laying bare the truth.

The truth of who we are.

Through whatever old wounds long forgotten.

Lying in a box pushed out of the light.

Waiting for the call.

To come into knowing.

And remember.

There are events in our lives, some big, some small, some irritating, some enlightening. The great tiny closet flood of '08 was all of these.

A pipe burst behind the wall of my utility closet turning a major storage area into a wading pool, water logging box after box of my hard to throw away unreviewed memory clutter.

After cursing through the disruption in my routine, I joggled through the cobwebs and disintegrated cardboard, breathing in the must of the untouched. It was unpleasant but I have to say, I found some peace in the clean up. I salvaged what I could from the soggy stew of box carnage, there wasn't much, a beautiful paper butterfly from some memorable event, a note from an old boyfriend that always made me smile, a few other mel-mentos here and there. By and large, it was almost a complete cleansing of the past.

Almost.

On the way to the trash bins an old hardcard Polaroid of adorable little me, at five years old, perfectly in tact, wholly clean of any flood damage, fell to the cement.

When you think Polaroid. You think moment in time. You've captured something, because you can hold it in your hand. Instantly. And. In many cases forever.

This moment held much more than that.

I always marveled at how this picture from childhood held a special place in my heart, evoking a charge of some kind. It was ethereal. I was leaning against a one rail fence, hair blowing, legs crossed, bare footed, flowing into an endless background of greens. It was a cool picture of a confident independent little girl.

In honor of its survival I put it on my desk, propped up against a green key jar. Where it sat, staring at me, until the day it decided to speak, just above a whisper.

"Turn me over"

Reaching across my desk to the hard thick old Polaroid, feeling heavy and at the same time significant. I flipped it over, revealing two handwritten words and a date.

LAKE TRIP (1972) over the faded factory printing: An Original Polaroid Land Photograph (printed in the USA)

Lightbulb. Spark. Recognition. Trauma.

There was a ripple in the air.

This was taken the day I drowned.

All the details rushed forward. Coloring into my mind.

I remembered the cabin. I remembered the lush blue green of the surf and sun in the Pocono Mountains of Pennsylvania. I remembered puttering along the lakeshore. I remembered chasing tadpoles toward the dock. I remembered being happily lost in a great place of fun and imagination and playing, seduced by the elusive tadpoles drifting further and further away from shore, edging deeper into the lake, until, the sandy floor started to sink beneath my feet.

I was caught. Stuck. In some whirlpooly quicksandy type soft spot in the earth. The more I panicked the worse it got. I was being dragged down.

I went under.

By the time anyone noticed, I was in trouble, struggling mightily, fighting for air.

Next thing I knew my mom was splashing next to me attempting a save.

To no avail.

We both went under.

I passed out as arms I would later find out were my father's pulled me and my mom to the shore.

Waking up. Blinking into focus. Lying in the dark on the bottom bunk of the cabin bedroom. The first thing I saw was wet money next to my dad's money clip on the bureau.

Scared and afraid. Trembling. I was alone. All I could think was I had almost killed my mother. I was responsible. In the future I'd have to be more careful. Really careful.

Blame fell down hard as I crashed into a fitful sleep, in which my over protective memory guard erased the whole event from my consciousness, leaving in its wake a dull ache, a fear of drowning, and a full blown case of feeling responsible. For everything.

Like many traumatic events too overwhelming to digest it was placed completely beyond my minds eye.

To wait.

Until the great tiny closet flood of '08 when it would emerge. To be faced. To be remembered. To be embraced.

As a piece of my history. A wound that wanted to be healed. Floating to the surface.

There was nothing I could have done. I wasn't responsible. I wasn't to blame. Everything had turned out alright. I mean. I'm alive. Right. My day dreaming, my humming, my drifting and playing wasn't wrong.

It was time to put my arms around that scared little girl who drifted off and almost lost her life. To let go of my fear. To let go of feeling responsible.

The memory just another puzzle piece revealing a treasure trove of acceptance. Another participant in my drama coming forward. Connected to the interlocking. Ever beginning and ending cycle of action and reaction and at long last being. All flowing to a beautiful tune. In a natural harmony of events. Letting go into the unseen. Spinning through the dance of oneness defining all the deepest parts of my self in wholeness.

The picture was a glowing calm, over a tempestuous memory that found its way to the surface. No longer wanting to stay underground.

To be integrated with my very foundation.

"Through the unknown, unremembered gate." (as TS Eliot wrote) Returning home. Creating a place and space of trust and support and revelation. "Arriving at my own door" available to me all along.

Home was within.

Home was without.

Home was here and now.

Home was everything that already was and always is.

There were so many chases and trips, and directions and events and places and experiments, and relationships all searching and never finding.

It wasn't anything I ever expected. It wasn't anywhere I expected it. Or with who. It didn't come into being by me doing anything. It simply existed within my heart space, when I could look at and be with and face my fear, knowing it was only an illusion to keep me from seeing the truth.

The truth of myself.

In love.

Eyes wide open.

Home.

Death

There comes a point in life where you can do nothing but destroy everything. My self esteem was in the toilet. There was nothing about myself that I liked. I couldn't trust anyone because I couldn't trust myself. I was in a ten year relationship and a marriage that wasn't working. After months and months of couple's therapy and years of trying to make it work. I was done. I walked out. It was over. I had failed. Miserably.

I looked around and saw happy families everywhere, and I couldn't touch, feel or go there. Time entered an endless and unbelievable pace of forever and fastidious sameness. To say I was alone is an understatement. I was isolated in a crowd. The universe engulfed me in a black hole of overwhelming knowledge out of my reach but ultimately within my understanding. Relationships melted away. Friends disappeared. There was no looking back. The Mel I had known died. The Couple Mel, the Accommodating Mel, the Friend

Mel, the Perfect Mel, the Nice and Agreeable Mel, the Smart Mel. Gone. Forever. The choice having been made was final. I was left with one thing. Move on.

I was terrified to let go. I knew I had no choice.

Death as a holiday. Death as a fun time.

Death as a journey.

Without a doubt, I'm different.

I killed myself and now I live.

Birth

I chased my first orgasm to London. As with every chase, it ended in disaster. He had a girlfriend. She was nice. As life would have it, we all ended up living together in a house near Hampstead Heath.

During those hours I was never more a stranger and, uncannily enough, never more at home. That encounter was the first of many in my life that drove home the unsettling but inescapable fact that we are all strangers in this world and that part of the elusive wonder of travel is that during those moments far away from all that is familiar, we are forced to face that truth, which is to say, the sacred truth of our soul's journey here on earth. This is one reason the stranger has always been held in awe and why the stranger on the move is perpetually a soul in wonder.
Phil Cousineau - The Art of the Pilgrimage

Late one luscious London evening, my Orgasm invited me into his room to give him a massage. The moon was full, and I was intrigued. I jumped at the opportunity in more ways than one. In the darkness of his bedroom and over the slight groans of his delight, my Catholic upbringing began to drum a thought into my head. "This isn't right." I could hear the Sunday School Nuns in their repetitive, monotonous voices amped with anxiety over souls on the verge of damnation chorusing, "NO!" The thought of his live-in girlfriend returning any moment was troublesome; but, I was on fire, energy pulsing through my body. I kept going. I wanted this to lead right down the road of no good. I moved my hands down his back feeling his energy, his skin, his everything, until I couldn't take it anymore. I did the only thing I could do. Panic. I made some awkward excuse that sounded like "hot dogs tomorrow" and busted out of the room, escaping to the seclusion of my bedroom. It was a short trip, just on the other side of the wall we shared. Then, I went to work.

I learned a lot that night. The least of which was how to masturbate. At 21, it was a long time coming. When the deed was done it was quite a satisfying accomplishment. I laid back into the darkness of that London night. I understood longing, self satisfaction, what owning self discovery could mean, and the beginnings of any complicated way of being in the world of love and lust.

Break Up

There are days where you can hardly believe anything. Divorce meant death. Death meant anxiety. Death meant darkness. Nobody really needs that.

It starts with the first steps, the idea that you can separate, and unravels from there like the thread on a favorite sweater. You ask yourself the question... "Can I do this? Is divorce an option?"

Where there was never a possibility of breaking up, somehow, the door pops open to the end of the relationship and the idea creeps over you that no matter what you do it will never work.

It is a notion at first. A thought flirting with you, not concrete and certainly its validity needing to be tested; to be showcased; to be tried; to be true. There are many reasons to hide or crush the thought of divorce; let's say you are in love; let's say you love your home, your friends, your rituals, your conversations. Hmmmm. What was wrong again? Stay focused.

I was with someone who didn't want the same things I did. Who was afraid of goals. Who was Twenty years older. Twenty years more rooted in bad patterns. Twenty years along the path of avoidance. Who should have been a friend but never my partner. He was short and cute and caught in a web of lies recycling through his families generations. Enough!

I had taken a temp job at one of the largest retail property groups in the world during this time of uncertainty, to help get some clarity, some distance, create a new perspective. I was a cog in an international machine. If you can't mow some endless lawn, this is the next best thing. Somewhat mindless structure 8:30am to 5:30pm every day. My office was on an upper floor in a designer high rise in Brentwood. The floor and the department in which I found myself was made up of 95% women, with all the quirks and eccentricities that are wonderfully wrapped in the collective consciousness of the female species. This island of solicitude on the ninth floor was filled with smiles, tears, disagreements and was to be my jumping off point. Between the cupcakes, birthdays, raffles, chats, lunches and work discussions I did what I had to do, gave myself time to think.

My personal struggles were obvious to everyone, my sadness just below the surface, my humor keeping a loose lid on my feelings. One of the girls cornered me in my office after a meeting about the future of the company's marketing plans had brought me to tears. In a voice just barely audible, I explained the decision pending about my marriage. She took a breath and shared with me her divorce story. She explained 'the worst part of a breakup is feeling like a failure.'

What! Huh!

Failure. Failure. Failure.

I was in my own collapsing zoom of realization. Failure. The word. It rang the bell. The evil terrible most hated word. Failure. That was it. I was exposed. I was overwhelmed with the thought of it. Failure. I didn't want to admit it. I didn't want to own it. I didn't want to be called a failure. I didn't want people to think I was a failure. I saw myself hanging on the 70% clearance rack, All Sales Final, with no interested parties. A design idea, sweated over, cared about and now ostracized in a mark down. I didn't want to admit that after all the years of effort and struggles I would come up empty. I didn't want to be a failure. But, I was.

The tears had no lid.

I needed time to think.

I headed to the roof.

I looked westward, into the bright and brilliant blue skies, across the Los Angeles horizon toward the ocean vistas and smiled. A truth was revealed. I knew. I was only going through the motions and the Herculean effort because I didn't want to admit I had failed.

Lorenz Hart & Richard Rogers standard This Can't Be Love started playing in my head. This can't be what love is about. This isn't what sharing your life is about. The drama I was in was not love. It wasn't even a clever disguise for love.

I had to leave my Man.

I not only knew it. I knew if I didn't, any hopes I had for the future I wanted would be destroyed forever. My ego had to take one for the team. For the greater good, in that moment, I admitted it. I owned it. I had failed. I began a mini celebration. Naming this long fought effort as a failure gave me momentary freedom from my troubles. What a spot to be in, a blip of joy, quickly muted by the fear of the future and what leaving my relationship would mean. I was fearful that I wouldn't have the courage to see it through.

I reprint an e-mail sent to a friend during this time.

I'm feeling fairly alone.
Saying it out loud to you, and getting the brain along the path, I've made a decision to move on.
He's so in avoidance or oblivion, hard for me to figure out what he is thinking if anything. I want things that I'm not getting out of the relationship and need. Can't be a bad thing to set some higher standards for myself, on communication, caring, support, goals etc.
My new friends, fear and sadness, are going to be cold comfort as winter approaches. And, I can't even think about what happens next. But, I'll have to figure it out, when I can think about it.
For now, I'm going to give myself a break.

It wasn't easy. My friend's response helped make the transition doable and in that moment gave me hope.

This is big, but we can do this. I know that saying this out loud can have a weird effect of making it real, like, there I said it, and I didn't fall into a black void and the world didn't stop spinning. So maybe I can do this thing that perhaps seemed totally undo-able before.

This is progress, painful as it may be.

Wanting things you are not getting out of your relationship - and being unwilling to settle for less - is hugely mature of you. I know you have asked for and tried to get these things and I am really proud of you for being willing to be so honest and do the hard work necessary to have the life you want.

You are not alone in this - please know I am just a phone call away. Reach out anytime you want to.

Take good care of you Mel - you are precious to all your friends who love you.

Progress. Painful. But progress.

"Reach out anytime." I was heard. I was encouraged and the path had been set. I just needed to follow it wherever it might lead. I had to let go of the "if only's" that repeated and repeated in my head. I had to let go of everything.

With the label of failure screaming through my being, knocking on every door it could. I still had to take the steps to leave.

I picked up the phone and scheduled a couple's therapy session. Would I be able to do it? Would I be able to say goodbye to everything I had known, any sense of security? It is amazing to realize even a painful, gut wrenching ache can feel like security, once you get used to it. Amazing that you could fear missing it. I never knew my security was false. I never knew I didn't feel safe. Would the pain and sadness be too much for me to get through? Did I have what it took?

I had no idea.

The only thing I did know. It was the only way. Take that first step.

I needed professional help. A professional to mediate. A professional to encourage the truth. A professional to strengthen any weakening sinews. There was no way I was going to enter the emotional waters of my relationship morass without a guide. I knew, going-in, this discussion with my man would probably be it, and to the very end, I provided him with the opportunity to rise to the occasion and do something to make amends.

Let's just say the meeting didn't go well.

I repeated what I wanted, and in absence of that, why I would be leaving. Why it was over. I wanted more than was being offered. I had been patient. I had asked over and over for what I wanted.

My Man was as dazed as ever. He didn't get it.

If you can believe it, my emotion of surprise at this fact caused me to lose my voice. I was hurt, insulted and speechless. The therapist carried the breakup ball across the finish line.

After the session, we drove home together in polite silence. In that silence, I picked the day I would move out. I closed the door on my old life. I pulled off this long, unhealing scab. Amazingly, I didn't disappear. It hurt like a bitch, but I was left with a feeling that my wounds could heal. That finding my voice would eventually redeem me.

The crying started and didn't end for a long time.

Tiny Lies

There are many reasons we fall under the spell of an untruth. I trapped myself under a lie, and I didn't know how to work my way out from under. I saw it happening. I made the bargain, and it nearly destroyed me.

My Man told me a month after we had moved in together, that it wasn't possible for him to have kids.

What!? Huh.

Did I hear him correctly? My Man couldn't have kids? I asked the obvious questions... "Why is this the first I'm hearing of this? Why didn't you tell me? Why have we been using condoms for months and months? And. How could you have a twelve year old son?"

Apparently, his son didn't know he was the product of an early sperm donation procedure. My Man and his Ex-Wife made a pact when their son was born never to share this information with him. To keep it entirely secret.

My Man went on to explain how he never knew why he couldn't get his former wife pregnant. After countless frustrations and disappointments of trying with no luck, finally his mom and dad came clean that there was an "accident" at birth.

My Man clearly and purposefully set out his fear-based boundaries and shared with me his desire to clutch tightly to his dishonesty. As he put it, "a storm was always threatening to roll in." I stepped into the liquid of his lie and sunk.

The constant terror and fear of anyone finding out about his son was now a tangible player in our relationship. He told me it was a secret I must keep. I felt his shame. I felt his fear. I felt compassion. I convinced myself it would be no big deal to not say anything. I leapt to his side of the fence. It's clear why I went there. I was in love. My Man was in pain. I could help.

I lost myself.

I never told anyone and held tight to his secret until it was too late. Odd. I never saw how I joined into his family's generational cycle of secrets.

More than anything, from our first date, I wanted to have my Man's baby. Weird. For ten years, I held out hope that one day a miracle would happen and my Man and I would be able to overcome his inability to have kids. I believed firmly, no matter what he said, something would happen and we would be blessed with a child. As the years ticked on, and I was met with nothing but a wall of anxiety, I needed to move the miracle along.

I changed paths.

Within five minutes of meeting a fertility doctor, all was

revealed. She asked me five questions. Five minutes. Five questions. At the end of our mini Q&A, to my surprise the miracle was possible. She explained to me my Man's condition and that we would be able to conceive. No problem. One of his testicles never descended; one of the "sacs" didn't drop when he was born, which the doctors treated like a vasectomy. That was the "accident" at birth. She assured me there were sperm floating around in "the boys" they just couldn't get out. Five minutes. Five minutes and all was revealed. No fear. No anxiety. Just hope. A decade of questioning disappeared. A decade of confusion was eradicated. There was a possibility. My long held dream of a baby with my Man sprang into prominence. I ran home and told my Man, who became immediately ill at ease, turning a whiter shade of pale. I was confused. I wasn't sure what was wrong, but I moved into action.

An armed woman is dangerous. I was now armed with information and ready to make it happen.

It didn't.

I was treated to one disrespectful tirade after tirade by my Man. He said the most unkind things one human being can say to another human being. He berated everything about me. He became angry, defensive and derogatory at the drop of a hat.

In very short order it became obvious, my Man didn't want to have a child with me. He had his son, now twenty one, and had been giving me lip service through the years. My therapist said something that would torment me. She called my Man an Unintentional Manipulator. Wow. An Unintentional Manipulator. I had always known his secret was more important than anything. I had hoped it wasn't more important than us.

I labored under false hopes for so long. I wasn't brave enough to face the truth until my face was rubbed in it repeatedly and I had exhausted every possible option. It was the ultimate "shame on me." The funniest part, for ten years I laughed off the comments about how cute our kids would be; I winced in secret at the repeated queries as to why my Man and his son looked nothing alike, and I avoided all in depth conversations about my child bearing plans. I had never told anyone the truth, how could I start now?

As many wonderful friendships developed and blossomed, I always had the secret, albeit his secret. I was trapped in it, a tiny lie that fouled the roots of every relationship I had.

Because I had engaged in a lie, not of my own making, there was always this barrier between me and everyone I came into relationship with. The closer I got to people, the worse it became. Kindness was a knife slicing into my lying soul. Support was a vindication of how unworthy I was. I didn't like myself, how could anyone like me? How could I love myself if I couldn't be honest with people who loved and trusted me? The vicious cycle had no end. I was sad for not being me, not being honest, not being respectful of my own needs. The wall became higher and thicker and more and more isolating. I always thought I had lived my life in doing the right thing. Clearly a fantasy. A double edged carcass left on the side of the road.

When you are lost, all feelings are rooted in the wrong sensors. Fusings of inappropriate emotions. Too bad. Love and support were complicated and extraordinarily out of my reach.

Never look back always be true
When it's all special
And nothings not true
You'll have found a life
That is precious to you.

Once you put yourself in the back seat, it's hard to get into the driver's seat, but I'd be damned if I didn't try. Bittersweet and yet. Necessary.

I could no longer live in the tiny lies. I had to find what was precious to me.

Roses

Very few people had any idea there were any difficulties or troubles with my Man, my relationship or my marriage. I never shared any details of the lie. I had made a bargain, and I staid the course.

When it was over it was over. There was no lead up of troubles. No discussions or requests of help. Just the appearance of normal times and then, no longer together.

The barriers I had created, the untruths that lived and breathed through my existence and my encounters stretched into long years of personal neglect and unspoken cries. There was a silent and unsurpassable rift between me and everyone I was in relationship with. The people I loved and respected and was closest to, I was cut off from. My own fear of disclosure, his ongoing secret, the pain and discomfort and distress had no bridge or way across. I desperately wanted to be heard, to be understood and explain the cause of my torment and pain. It wasn't to be. I was tongue tied and fear encrusted and holding onto my role with a death grip.

I was a tough customer. I could take it. I told myself. The tougher it was the stronger I became, and the more I would be rewarded at some future date. Well, that future date never came.

His battle cry for my place in his drama and his fear was "this is who I am, accept me."

> *I won't send roses,*
> *or hold the door*
> *I won't remember*
> *which dress you wore*
> *My heart is too much in control*
> *The lack of romance in my soul*
> *Will turn you grey, kid*
> *So stay away, kid*

When one Friday afternoon, I was drawn to the Mack and Mabel 1974 cast album starring Robert Preston and Bernadette Peters, I lost it. The song relates an older Mack Sennett explaining to a young, infatuated Mabel Normand what a relationship with him would mean. Jerry Herman summed up the sentiments beautifully.

> *Forget my shoulder,*
> *when you're in need*
> *Forgetting birthdays*
> *is guaranteed*

And should I love you,
you would be
The last to know
I won't send roses,
and roses suit you so
With words romantic
I'm at a loss
I'd be the first one to agree
That I'm preoccupied with me
And it's inbred, kid
So keep your head, kid
In me you'll find things
Like guts and nerve
But not the kind of things
That you deserve
And so while there's a fighting chance
Just turn and go
I won't send roses
And roses suit you so.

My Man could have sung this song. Could have been that guy. He was older. He was damaged. He was a tortured, cemented soul parading around in an accommodating nice guy performance suit. Oblivious to his fatal flaws, but draped in them.

There it was.

Herman's deft lyrics play out the emotion of an infatuated Mabel, entering the bargain and accepting what is offered with no thought to what the choice will mean in the future. Giving up on roses.

So who needs roses
Or stuff like that
So who wants chocolates
They'd make me fat
And I can get along just fine
Without a gushing Valentine
And I'll get by, kid
With just the guy, kid
And though I know I may be left
Out on a limb
So who needs roses
That didn't come from him.

I related immediately. I agreed early in my relationship with my Man that I would not need roses.

I wouldn't need any of it.

The mistake of accepting less than you need and convincing yourself you would be fine was the ultimate heartbreaker. I was left out on a limb of my own choosing. Good luck getting off the limb without the fire department, the S.W.A.T rescue team and every known form of coaxing you could find.

I was young. I didn't understand the bargain I had made. I didn't understand the choice I had given up, and I didn't understand how it would betray me. I was caught up in the youth and rapture of being in love. It took a long time to release the recriminations.

So who needs roses.

The Lobster Room

The Lobster Room was the first stop on my road to reclaim Mel outside of my relationship of ten years. Leaving everything I knew behind took major support and help, but most importantly, it took having a place to go.

I started the pilgrimage into the unknown at the home of a friend with an extra room and a generous spirit. The Lobster Room with its cheery reddish color and Maine Lobster motif, was a complete New England cottage like room, down to fine art sketches of crustacean covering the walls.

The parade of grief had begun.

I would refer to The Lobster Room as the womb. The womb caught the sun in the morning, had its own bathroom, was isolated in its own wing of the house and couldn't have been a more comfortable place to weep.

Having lived a life free of accepting unconditional support, this step might seem unfathomable. I tell you it would never have entered my mind as a possibility pre-break up, but desperate times called for desperate measures, and post breakup there was no question I needed help. All kinds of help. I jumped out of my home, my marriage and all that I knew and landed in the Lobster Room. Looking back, I could have done a lot worse for myself.

Kindness comes in many packages, and I needed to learn how to open them up.

There is no question I grew in the Lobster Room. The womb was restorative. I perched myself in my despair, boiled some water, enjoyed the comforts of cup after cup of tea and got through Phase One of the mess that was my existential broken existence. My friend and owner of The Lobster Room, would deposit reading material on the bed in the evenings. A seemingly endless supply of self help books obtained from the "library" of discarded books at the YMCA. This rickety, overflowing cart of entertainment always reminded me of the Island of Misfit Toys from a favorite Christmas claymation special, tattered but with a lot of heart. This wasn't your normal self help, this was a pageant of self help starting in the 60's racing to the 80's. It wasn't current or cutting edge but page by page, it informed my development, it created a wall of support that could shore up whatever troubles would threaten to overwhelm me.

Truths are truths no matter what era they come from. I loved the 70's book that suggested you sleep with the first attractive man that crossed your path. It propagandized that having sex was a great step toward cutting emotional ties and moving on from the old relationship. The only road block on this one was having to interact with the opposite sex. I wasn't ready.

I lived an examined life in the womb and buried myself into this time capsule of psychoanalysis, letting go and heart break. I wish I could remember all of the titles. I gratefully returned them to the "library" at the YMCA when I was finished. I did keep two of the books from this phase. Leo Buscaglia's 1982 masterpiece that was a collection from his lectures entitled, Living, Loving & Learning, and a book I actually purchased called Spiritual Divorce by Debbie Ford.

Leo hit it squarely on the head... "An investment in life is an investment in change. We've got to learn to trust again, to believe again. Of course, it's a risk, but everything is a risk. We need to begin to go beyond just 'being' again. We've got to get in touch with being human."

Go Leo. And Go Mel!

I adopted a new theme song. This time, Open a New Window from Jerry Herman's Mame.

> *Simply travel a new highway,*
> *Dance to a new rhythm,*
> *Open a new window ev'ry day!*

The Lobster Room was a beacon, a lighthouse in my breakup that guided me to the safety of the shore. After being emotionally adrift, it was nice to feel my feet touch ground. I was ready to open a new window.

It was time to move on. I had to rip myself out of the Lobster Room and the safety that was the womb. I forced myself to move on. It needed to be done.

The Monk

The answer to the question, "Who's there when you emerge from the cave or in my case the womb of the Lobster Room?" had a twist. You are working through the pain and the sadness and always the letting go. It's amazing how many things you need to let go of. What isn't serving you. You know it's all for the best but it doesn't feel very good. This is raw stuff so you have paper thin defenses. In this emergent reality, a man's path crossed mine. He happened to be a Monk. He happened to be a rebel Monk. A rebel Monk from a contemplative monastic order, who had spent 35 years of his life devoted to the study, exploration and the concepts of self.

He was sabbaticalized and given a year to think about what a dark force he had become against the existing self realization infrastructure. His talks had become dangerous and his questions deafening. Self realization was about the self realizing things -- not following a guru... Right? A strapping twenty years old when entering the monkhood, now living on the outside at fifty five, he was naive to the ways of many of life's details while being a wizened master and sharp student of humanity.

The Monk is a straight talking truth teller. He had lived his life advising many high level folks on spirituality and truth, while living his own long quest to achieve universal answers. He had dissected the world and then pieced it back together free from patterns, prejudices and programming. Over the years, he became an advisor, a confidant, a friend to many famous and enlightened individuals. A mix of sage and survivor. He is a special man, with a unique mind. I don't know how he came into my life. It happened. I went with it. What a delightful encounter. What a life changing place in my timeline to run into the Monk.

The Monk and I had many discussions and shared a deep familial sensibility. Comfortable and dangerously informed of each other's plights with very little exchange. It was nerve wracking in its intensity. It was instant and simple. We were brothers and sisters and friends destined to light a small path out of our respective darkness.

We kicked off each of our dissertations and times together by making a pot of coffee. Coffee being a stimulant of original thought became the perfect beginning to our conversations. Making something, albeit something as simple as a pot of coffee, created a buffer to the intensity that would follow. Plus it sharpened the wits, and brightened the senses, necessary for any conversation with the Monk.

All I've ever wanted to do was fit in. Feel a sense of

belonging with others. The Monk saw right away this was a metropolitan vanity. A thing which was fanciful and ridiculous and down a wayward path of unanswered wonderings that would never be fulfilled. My answers were not going to come from idle chit chat and misdirected energies and exhaustive quests. I wasn't asking myself the important questions. Fitting in was for fools lost in the belief of belonging. Peeling back the onion of understanding involved examining those beliefs. The Monk set about gently blowing my mind with ideas and options.

If I hadn't picked my new path, I would never have encountered this teacher. Never before had I met anyone like him. The timely meeting of the Monk, a soul kindred to mine, along my trek down the universal way was perfection. The student was ready and the master appeared. In doses small and large, we spent months together working and pushing and stretching the boundaries of polite chatter into new arenas of discovery.

We got in fights. At times he irritated me; at times he made me laugh; at times he illuminated thoughts that planted seeds of permanent change while rooting me into myself. It was frustrating, but I kept at the discovery.

Something strange about the Monk. I brought him up in all my conversations, shared his wisdom with others and tried to explain to people who the Monk was and what he meant to me. People didn't seem to get it. It was for me to understand, for me to transition. My Monk. My time. As quickly as he appeared, he was out of my life. It came to an end. He left me with the following journal entry.

MY MATINEE IDOL MEL

Once upon a very temporary time, we were tempted to believe the longitude and latitude of so many untold things. Our reasoned reality and small - world, someday - rapture was something far far from experience, and so we built a life on land, east of the horizon, and began reading books on heroes, heresy and hope. Thus, was bliss renounced for blasphemy, the present becoming but the price of horizoned tomorrow, and we - the good and bad, the children - of no - choice, were left to voice our vicious truth through appropriate and authorized channels-of no change. But we have survived success. We have played the fantasy game of narrow all-but-now. But something happened along the Chevron way. The myth busted, the carrot-future never came. The dream was seen... leaving an inspired sub-liminal dementia, where minds must die to their half-truths and too, too tangible attachments of living happily ever after!

The noble ever-new of now is the most raucous fear my unowned (worried) mind can part the closed curtain for. The thought of presence is too powerful for one who has lived (if that's the word) in per-petual post-ponement and per-formance. For I have rejected good with bad. I have exhausted both head and wounded heart. All I dare expect is left is the pure intentionality of... surrender... to the event-horizon people like us have quite determined to sail over, to fatefully follow the westering light that leads to the far, far east. After a linear struggle to somewhere, looking for the myth in one too many, what would happen, dear defiant gypsy, if we suddenly stopped our journey? What if we became reluctant saints and let our quixotic (perhaps projected) gods seek us? My money tells me - that the whole uni-verse would scroll like an infinited and surfeited newly tamed pet... at our

newly-powerful, but perhaps still-petulant feet! Reverse-psychology
has its own diverse appeal, and as I said
the other day, I now know it... all... comes... down... to
... this!
The only value
is validating
the divinity
in the division.
Thus, we are the Ones, the One, we've been waiting for, the
angry, crazy, begging, and supremely dangerous gods!
Sorry, Mel, it was all a myth, a movie, a mania that we (who
else?) ... co-created PRODUCED AND PROJECTED...
By my matinee idol Mel....

I didn't open up my journal to read his thoughts until weeks after our final Friday conversation. I couldn't.

When I did read it, I could barely turn through the pages or grasp its meaning and when I was finished I closed it quickly feeling dissected and not comforted or warm and fuzzy.

I still jump when I see 'dear, defiant, gypsy' it strikes me as a seeing, a knowing of my wills and dreams and spirit. A long dance of tomorrow that never found today.

Now, months after our final meeting and conversation, several things spring out at me. I'll point them out for the sheer joy that comes when something leaps off the page and becomes a mirror to realizations, quieting and answering that long beckoning question that begins the first time we look in the mirror and try to recognize self, asking, "Who is that woman in the mirror?"

I had no reason to rush everything along, speeding through life to what was next. The Monk made that clear. Everything in its time and time heals everything.

"We survived success... the dream was seen.... leaving an inspired sub-liminal dementia, where minds must die to their half truths and too, too tangible attachments of living happily ever after!"

Happily Ever After, ugh. Such a complex concept. I have struggled with this since the many fairy tales and books I absorbed as a child. Our need for magic, our desire to have some meaning or knowing of the meaning of our lives and how it would turn out. Fairly tales always had a happy ending.

The Monk's words lingered. Happily Ever After.

Stephen Sondheim again leaps to mind. He's explored this concept of Happily Ever After in a number of his songs and an entire show Into the Woods. Sondheim deals with what happens after the myth, after the dementia, with a sour note of regret and impossibility and always hope.

> *Why should you sweat, what do you get?*
> *One day of grateful for six of regret.*
> *Someone to hold you to close*
> *someone to hurt you to deep*
> *Someone to bore you to death,*
> *Happily ever after!*
> *That's Happily Ever After*
> *So quick,*
> *Get a little car,*
> *take a little drive,*

make a little love,
do a little work,
take a little walk
You've got one little trip,
Seventy years, spread it around
Show a little feeling
why should you try
why not try
sure feel a little lonely
but fly
why not fly.
That's happily ever after,
ever ever after, for now.

A long, epic idea was at last coming to some conclusion. The bullfighter in me was ready to head out to dinner and give the bull a rest. Happily Ever After can have a lot of meaning and a lot of possibilities. The definition does not have to involve a prince and riding into the sunset. Many endings were possible. It was a choice.

All that seemed wrong
was now right, and those who deserved to
were certain to live a long and happy life.
Ever after.

I was beginning to grasp that I could reach a part of myself and connect my intellect to my feelings and yearnings. I could feel and speak and soar.

"Life is anyone's guess, a constant surprise."

Ever changed, ever questioning, at last content....

Happily Ever After? Not quite. But closer.

> *Witches can be right,*
> *Giants can be good.*
> *You decide what's right*
> *You decide what's good*
> *You decide alone*
> *But no one is alone.*

I was amazed by the unusual and miraculously life affirming way the universe kept putting things, people, events, occurrences in my path, allowing me to experience just what I needed when I needed it.

Even though the Monk was gone, he taught me that not only do we need a mirror to our growth and formation but also a reference marker to who we might become if we let go of the fantasies, good and bad. Ever After.

Collateral Damage

To save myself I needed to break up with my Man, leave my home and start over. I had no idea it would lead to the loss of so many people I called my friends and considered my family.

The lineup of bodies was long and strong. People would ask about so and so, and I'd shrug into the inevitable head shaking responses: "Haven't emailed me back," "Not speaking to me," "Not talking to them," "Not calling them," "Not returning my call," "Haven't spoken to them," or my personal favorite, "They are getting a restraining order against me," to be met with the shock of judgement that would escape from their lips, "Them too?" All I could do was nod. Yep. Gone. Not forgotten but no longer of the Mel Universe.

Through no fault of anyone, through no explanation or ill will in what went down, sides have to be chosen in a breakup. Very few people can maintain a relationship that lives on both sides. It takes a special individual to straddle the fence and separate allegiances. It's the extra effort that many people don't want to make and given the state of the Mel Union, next to impossible. Failure is uncomfortable all the way around. A breakup is awkward, emotionally volatile, and can be irritating and irrational and shattering for all involved.

We all want to be liked and accepted. We all want to know that no matter what, we will still be liked and accepted. I was left bruised and incomplete and wholly unliked by the only person who mattered. Me.

My mirror was cracked. I could hardly recognize the person I was in the eyes of the people that surrounded me. I was a collection of jagged edges. Jagged edges all wanting to be liked and accepted. Not a good place to be.

Throughout my cloak of low self esteem, I had thought the only way to be liked was to People Please. To a certain extent I was a born People Pleaser. A sensitive, sincere soul trying to be helpful.

People Pleasing works. People Pleasing builds and builds and builds, filling stadiums full of fluffers, noodlers, fallacies and fantasies.

Stopping People Pleasing brings you to your friends.

When you pull the plug and break up a marriage, you can only deal with so much. Everything becomes very simple because it has to. You can't get caught in drama, or other's issues, or other's needs for you; you can only focus on what you need to get through the day. Then, once you are getting through the day, you can begin to focus on what you want. And you want to be better. You want to forgive yourself for the perceived mistakes you have made. You want to have some understanding of what happened and most importantly, you want to be surrounded by love and support. Anything that doesn't feed this, needs to go. No matter how lonely or down or tough it is. You must walk into the fire and know you will come out the other side. This is how life works. Beds of crap need to be slept in, and you need to wake up, clean yourself off and get through. This movement toward "no pain" isn't good. Pain helps you. It is part of the healing process. "It takes courage to change patterns of denial, for we must be willing to let things get worse before it gets better."

Things definitely got worse.

As I changed, my relationships changed. As I stopped People Pleasing, as I asked for more, as I explained what I wanted, what I needed, things shifted. Rebuilding meant loss. Hand in hand. I couldn't be afraid of it anymore.

"Am I the only one left from your bridal shower?" a friend laughingly mentioned one afternoon. I laughed with her. Ridiculous. But, Agatha Christie's And Then There Were None flew into my brain.

There was a lovely photo from my bridal shower: of the twelve people in the picture, three made it through my breakup. A ratio of seventy percent loss. High? Maybe, but by the time the marriage came to an end, I was pretty messed up.

The losses suffered made way for discovery.

My close friend who hosted my bridal shower was one of the first people I told of my Man's secret and not only did she not beat me down, she extended a shoulder and helped me know I needed more from those I was closest to and planned on spending my life with.

This friend served me until she didn't.

> *I called a thousand times*
> *I wrote a thousand words*
> *I shared a thousand thoughts*
> *And only wanted more*

I played out my franticness at this friend's loss until I was healed. I did what I needed to do for me. Let's just say we had different experiences of what went down.

When we were done. We were done.

This loss was important as waking up is important.

I felt like Katharine Hepburn forever transformed by a friend's suicide in the final scenes of Stage Door, "The calla lilies are in bloom again. Such a strange flower, suitable to any occasion. I carried them on my wedding day, and now I place them here in memory of something that has died."

Those who remained adapted, communicated and joined me on the other side. They accepted my clumsy attempts to regain my footing free of the People Pleasing, free of the frills, the mania and the fantastical illusion.

The more I healed, the fewer jagged edges and the more space opened up for people to meet me.

Samuel Johnson said, "Life has no pleasure higher or nobler than friendship." I always thought I had a lot of friends.

There's a wonderful description from Bruno Bettelheim in The Uses of Enchantment: The Meaning and Importance of Fairy Tales. " Struggle against severe difficulties in life is unavoidable. Is an intrinsic part of human existence -- if one does not shy away, but steadfastly meets unexpected and often unjust hardships, one masters all obstacles and in the end emerges victorious."

> *Time took us for granted*
> *then played us a fool*
> *I've never forgotten*
> *And always been true*

It doesn't take a stadium full of supporters to get you through, it only takes one.

I had some friends and now they are gone.

Nourishment

I knew I was malnourished. My confusion over the patterns that had unwittingly developed surrounded me. I had depleted my resources. I had been slowly and unwittingly destroying parts of myself. I would now need to address areas that had long been neglected.

I have some of the strangest cravings, I always have. These cravings began and ended with food. Food. A constant source of inspiration and brain energy. Food. A love. A passion. An endeavor. An eternal and ever glowing light of satisfaction. To me, finding the perfect meal is as central to life as breathing. Everything I did revolved around when we will eat, where we would eat, what the best snack might be, what was the perfect food to go with a jazz evening. Was two in the morning the perfect time to grab a hot dog with mustard and onions after a friend's party?

I set about all kinds of ways to learn about food. Top chefs, restaurants, gourmet cooking clubs... I cooked and read and learned, had dinner parties, invited friends over, explored and experimented. I knew how to satisfy my hunger. I understood food was love. It was a creative quest, a noble endeavor. When going downtown to see Ibsen's Enemy of the People, Persian food with a dry Asian beer. The mix of cultures combined with Ibsen's questioning of a society's morality and integrity. Fabulous. What better accompaniment to a man standing up to a town leadership and being labeled the Enemy of the People for his troubles? Practice made perfect. A slice of pizza from Mama Lido's when comforting a friend over a recent breakup. Something about the greasy cheese that loosens the barriers and gets closer to the core, easing some of the pain. Island burger with chips and salsa before or after a Christopher Guest movie. Try it. Many combinations work. Abstract pairings - fun. I will tell you, some don't work and can cause late night discomfort, but you overlook these missteps on the way to the satisfaction of the perfect pairing, taking the experience to a richer level, layering and nuancing the ideas explored and expressed during an outing. I'll say it again. Try it. Comfort was a huge part of my feelings. I was feeding my hunger, sure, but there was something more, I was practicing a long honored tradition of nourishing some need, some part of myself. Nourishment. Nourishing. To nourish a part of myself. Hmmmm, there was something here.

No matter how far you've come, how long you've been on this earth, things can scare the shit out of you. There is nothing more terrifying than the idea of throwing a big meaty steak at a ferocious starving lion that hasn't had any meat for years.

What was starving in some deep cave of my being that needed to be fed? How violent would that part of me be when I started to address it? I knew there was a part of myself that wasn't being fed, that wasn't getting its spotlight, that was starving. I had no idea what long tucked away Mel was being tortured or where she lurked in my subconscious, but I knew for sure there was much of myself unaddressed, some long suffering, unfed parts of myself that would need some attention and care and feeding. I wouldn't be able to just chuck some meat into the cave. I'd have to come up with a way to systematically and continually find and feed the beast and maintain a consistency that wouldn't repeat the deprivation that had caused panic and distress and confusion for so many years.

Realization can be terrifying, but a new path had opened up. I was missing something. Missing something very dearly, and I became curious and excited by ideas of what would nourish me.

An acquaintance of mine shared a story and led me in a new direction on nourishment. She felt that her family had never accepted her chosen path in life, didn't encourage her on any level. She sought comfort in therapy only to be derided by family members with their chorus of "Are you still in therapy?" Her translation... "Are you still fucked up?" The time came when she was starring in Tennessee Williams, The Rose Tattoo, and she knew what she needed, and she finally asked for it. In a polite note to her family, she requested they send flowers opening night and for the run of the show. Every day flowers showed up at the theater with a note that said, "We are proud of you." The flowers fed her, nourished the dream she held for so long, night after night, the flowers told the story of acceptance. She related how nourished she felt by the very sight of the flowers. When the show closed, for the first time in her life she felt full.

Note to Mel: Revelation. Nourishment could mean many different things. Food wasn't the only item that could be nourishing. Nourishment could be applied to self, needs, desires, feelings, wants, ideas, you name it. This concept blipped so strongly on my radar, the signal growing stronger and stronger with each passing second. Beckoning long forgotten parts of myself. Nourish yourself. Do it. Now.

Nourishment. Wow. I had never fully opened myself up to the concept. I didn't get how powerful a concept this would be. I didn't know what would feed me, but if I was quiet and listened maybe all would be revealed.

Back to the basics. I had spent much of my life supporting others. The role I had assumed was as an encourager. A supporter. An inspirer. A People Pleaser. A booster of confidence for everyone I met or came in contact with. You can do it. You can get everything you want. Your dreams can come true. I was trying and pushing with every fiber of my being to feed some part of myself by pointing the light outward. I would need to turn the light back on myself and get busy. I needed to be my own cheerleader. A quarterback for all that life could be. I needed to stand in my own life and call the shots, to revel in the spotlight and shine.

No more would I be afraid to be as big as I could be, no more would I live and breathe in the shadows.

The path forward kept opening up in front of me, and I

would follow it. Follow the light. Wherever it might lead.

When the lights go on. It's amazing what you can see. How interesting. I was doing and acting out what I was looking for myself. I spent all of my fuel on others. Using my new word, I was spending so much time nourishing others in hopes that some of it would filter back to me, I had nothing left. How could I do the work, make the effort, correct the behavior, calm the distress, and reach "feeling fed" if I was exhausted?

Wait. "Put one foot in front of the other."

I was ready.

I started small. Massage, trust, sharing, surprise happy notes to myself, hikes, asking for what I needed, biting my tongue when people offered help, sitting on my hands when false distress signals erupted onto the scene.

The path seemed long; the time to the fabricated finish line would keep growing with no end in sight.

As I slowly began to recharge, cooking and food lost its sheen. I didn't want to go out to dinner; I didn't want to do anything that involved the ritual of food. Cheap eats were fine. I called it Fast Food Open Season. Chicken wings. Yum! Bring it on. I chose to spend my energy on new areas of nourishment. Exploring and expanding and experimenting with what fueled the me I was becoming. When a dear friend invited me to a Memorial Day weekend get together and was excited about having a 'cook fest' I immediately responded with, "I'd love to come, but it will be impossible for me to cook. I'll pick something up."

What the hell was wrong with me? Why was cooking such an evil, awful sorrowful thought in my head? Why did I want to avoid it at all costs? Food was a function of nourishment, after all. There was only one thing I could do. The Mel Stare Fest. Look closer. In extreme close up, the horror of looking at myself from any realistic distance is mitigated. I would stand very close to the mirror and stare at myself until the answers choked themselves out. They did. The realization that I was alone. No one was around me. I had only myself to take care of. I could cook for no one. What had seemed so comforting for so long was replaced with the real nourishment of taking care of myself.

I didn't want to go back to the old me and was afraid that picking up an old habit like cooking would hurt me. It was an amazing moment. I was concentrating on feeding the bigger part of myself, that forgotten-along-the-way, still-unknownto- me-stranger, who was the part of myself crying out for help. Food had needed to take a break from the action while I focused on me.

Sondheim delivered the idea. The moment. The realization. Looking in the mirror. Understanding. From his show Follies.

> *Who's that woman?*
> *I know I know that woman,*
> *So clever, but ever so sad.*
> *Love, she said, was a fad.*
> *The kind of love that she couldn't make fun of*
> *She'd have none of.*
> *Who's that woman.*
> *That cheery, weary woman*
> *Who's dressing for yet one more spree?*

Each day I see her pass

In my looking-glass--

Lord, Lord, Lord, that woman is me!

I had me. To cook for, to live for. I did want to cook, I just didn't want to get burned anymore. When I had completed the healing and nourishment of all parts of myself, I would have a feast. Until then, I wouldn't cook for others until I felt more complete than incomplete. When I felt full, I would head back to the kitchen. It was such a satisfying thought, with each breath it became more and more possible that not only would this happen, there would also eventually be that someone special that I could cook for. I hadn't met him, I hadn't experienced him, but he was out there, out there waiting for the moment when our eyes would meet. It would all be there once I learned to take care of myself, to set my own table with everything necessary to fuel my tanks. From now on. It was on. I allowed myself to hope I could retrain myself. I was on a path. A path of nourishing the starved pieces of myself with a new and powerful knowing that I could emerge whole, fed, and grounded with the ability to recognize a need and how to nourish it.

I was oh so grateful for the path that had opened in front of me and started to look forward to the day when I would have a feast.

.

Disclosure

There's no announcement card or email greeting you can order and send out that says, "Hope all is well. I'm getting a divorce! I'm going to go through months and months of horrific hideousness, call me."

Announcing a separation or divorce is awkward. No way around it. Talking about it not one of the hot topics on the everyday agenda. You don't feel like bringing it up. You let it go in the response to someone's casual "What's going on?" You don't respond when people tell you, "Say hello to your Man for me." You just don't get into it. People have no clue. You don't want to go into some long explanation. Nobody needs it. When you do feel compelled to say something, you eventually stammer out "um, well. We're not together anymore," then simmer through explanations that you are tired of hearing.

One day you get a bit angry with yourself for not wanting to deal with it, and you blurt out to strangers and everyone you run into, "I'm getting a divorce."

This was my first email attempt at an explanation in response to a, "Say hello to your Man for me":

Darlin'

How are the monkeys doing? It is a nice surprise to get your email. How are you?

On my front, this is a little awkward to announce over email... my Man and I are no longer together. I moved out.

Never really been through a heartbreaker, so I'm a little shell shocked by the constant hum of sadness.

We started couple's therapy in April and things worked themselves out to the realization I wasn't in the right relationship. I faced a ton of shit I was scared to get an answer to and the answers were exactly what I was afraid of. Ugh.

It's a bit of a start over. A foundation rebuild if you will... I haven't been able to talk about it with many people... I've kind of set up an inner and outer circle on the friends front. Emotionally it is a raw and vulnerable time. The weeping can start at anytime, sister, as I found out while watching the farrelly bros comedy fever pitch and in my yoga class. Yikes.

Her response helped me to release a long pent up breath I had been holding:

Not the best opening line... but I'm not disappointed in the outcome of your current situation. I actually think this is a good move for you.

Granted, it's always sad to separate from a confidant, or

anyone for that matter you promise to cherish… but I wasn't

entirely convinced that the relationship was the right

relationship for you. So, I have mixed emotions of sorrow and

excitement for what the future holds in store for you and the

next adventure you will soon be on.

Brutal honesty will bring sun and in it will be many rewards

offering assurance that your are on the right path. It just

may not feel like that now, and that's okay. Better to feel

something…

Expect a picture of the monkeys to brighten your fridge.

And, of course; I'm here.

No longer were tears falling into a cold night. It got easier
to handle the varied responses as it got easier to announce and
dismiss the disclosure of getting a divorce, finally moving to
the shorthand…

"I'm joining the divorce party, give me a hug."

Until Hallmark and Miss Manners collaborate on a "How
to" etiquette book rivaling the ritual of getting married, I
recommend cutting to the chase.

Searching

The children's book Are You My Mother? showcases a baby bird that hatches while his mother is away. He sets out to look for her and asks everyone he meets, "Are you my mother?"

It happens. You have the mother you have.

My mother's first words on hearing about the separation from my Man were "I told you so." She said it with such relish that it felt like she had been waiting the whole of the ten years to decry my mistaken union. The fact that she was right. Erked me like you can't believe.

Several good friends related their shock when spending a little talk time chatting with my mother that she didn't ring my praises. She didn't offer nice remembrances. Instead, she focused her time on how I had never done anything she thought I should, how I never turned out how she wanted me to turn out. That I never made it easy, never liked anything that she liked. My friends couldn't believe they didn't get some adorable story about how cute I was or how cool I was, or how charming it was that I wore the same striped turtleneck for months or ran naked around the neighborhood after reading a story about the forest sprites. They couldn't believe my mother would take the opportunity to, as they put it, "bash me."

I was used to it. I had long ago accepted the disapproving disappointment, the begrudging belittlement and the bemoaning behaviors. It fueled my belief there was something wrong with me and lent credibility to my theory that I was never going to be good enough.

My mother wanted a doll, a best friend, a kindred spirit, a patsy to her whims, someone to bring her happiness and fulfillment. She forced me into perms, beauty shops. Always the comment, "Why can't you be more like a girl?" One of her favorite refrains: "If only you could be more like a cheerleader." "Why don't you want to do this?" "Stand there and take it." "Isn't this bedazzling gorgeous?" NO! It isn't. Agggggh. I wanted to run. I felt tortured. As I write this I can't say I didn't and don't like wearing dresses. I did. I do. My taste was just on the opposite pole from my mother's. She liked fru fru. I liked tailored, Chanel, classic. Her cloth's colors and my colors never matched.

The wallpaper in my room growing up had tiny lavender flowers and was accented in lavender. I liked my room. It was lovely. That said, it didn't mean I wanted to wear purple. That fact seemed as obvious to me as the sun rising every day. It didn't stop the silk purple shorts suit that was gifted to me on a particularly difficult Christmas. It was expensive. It was hideous. And I had it, until the day I walked out of my marriage, when my friend assembled twenty bags of niceties I couldn't let go of, now going to Good Will.

I don't remember so many things. I do remember the inexplicable ache that never went away. The change in my breathing that occurred when confronting something I couldn't place. I do remember never feeling safe.

We all need a shoulder, a place to feel comforted. To be as old as I was without that shoulder was interesting.

There is a line I remember hearing from a comedienne talking about how she finally got to a place where she could have a relationship with her mom... "We've come to an understanding. We've agreed. We're not going to understand each other."

In that understanding, I could stop searching and let go.

Mow the Lawn

I was barely getting through the days when a development job came open. It was an entry level position; it was way below my usual salary; it was something I could do with very little effort. I took it.

During a fairly intense meeting discussing and planning The Last and Best Year of Your Life, a project inspired by George Harrison's battle and untimely death from cancer, I was lost in a daydream. What would you do if you were given a death sentence? A year to live. Harrison's words, "It reminds you that anything can happen," sailed into my consciousness.

After the meeting, one of the wise souls in attendance stayed behind to chat. We got into the most interesting conversation. This angel shared with me a story. A story I will remember for the rest of my life.

After huge success, he had lost everything. He lied, cheated, alienated and destroyed everyone and everything that he came in contact with. Left with nothing and no one, he returned home to a small town in Arkansas, took a job on a construction crew in a growing development, his only place to sleep a rented car.

Over and over, he asked himself one question, "Am I crazy?" In his mind only a crazy person would have lied and dishonored himself in the manner which he chose. He couldn't go on until he answered his crying soul's question of sanity. With a foundation only a steady paycheck can bring, he moved out of his car into an apartment and was ready to face the music.

One rainy day, work was canceled. He drove the short distance to the town's state-funded mental institution, went to the receptionist and said, "I need to speak to the toughest psychologist you have on staff." After several back and forths, he was told to grab a seat. As he sat in the waiting room, he made a promise to himself. He would tell the truth. He would tell the truth and face the bleakest of places the human soul can go. He would find out if he was crazy.

Sitting before the psychiatrist, he poured out every last detail of his scandalous behavior. He told the truth. For the first time in his life, his blackness had a voice.

"Doc, am I crazy?"

The psychiatrist didn't respond, but instead asked him to take a test and evaluation and return to the institution his next day off. Exhausted from the effort of revealing himself, he filled out the questionnaire and test without thinking, just filled in the first answer that came to his mind. If he was crazy, he sure as hell wanted to know and scheduled his next appointment for Saturday.

When Saturday came, the psychiatrist informed him that he was most certainly not crazy. Although his tests showed his tenacity to be off the charts, he never gave up on anything.

The psychiatrist prescribed the following... Go back to your job on the construction crew. Do not slack off. Do not accept any additional responsibilities. Do not excel. Be average. Mow the lawn. Do your job. You will know when it is time to move on.

Day in and day out he did just that, he mowed the lawn. For months he turned down additional responsibilities, pay raises, promotions and just did what needed to be done. With his prescription and direction, he felt no compunction or anxiety that he wasn't doing enough.

One day. Eleven months into his job, he was done mowing the lawn. He felt right with himself.

After sharing this story, he stood before me, a true success. A man changed by having gone through something incredibly tough, facing it in his own unique way and learning one of the best lessons life can offer. Mow the lawn until you don't need to mow the lawn anymore.

Sister Friends

I had two brothers growing up in a neighborhood of all boys. I gravitated to their activities, running, playing, football, baseball. I wanted to be like them. Adventurous. Free.

The one girl who lived in "The Circle" where I grew up wasn't cool. She may even have had some emotional problems, I don't know. My only memory of trying to hang out with her was when she got a new puppy. She wanted to show it off. Unfortunately, she thought the little guy could "run" along as she biked with its leash tied unmercifully to the handlebar. I watched as she pulled then dragged the little terrified pup unable to keep up with her bike. The puppy's only option was surrender, to give in and slide its body along the pavement. Horrible.

I mention this because being a tomboy doesn't lend itself to relating to girls, dolls, dresses, shopping, chit chatting. None of it was on the agenda, much to the chagrin of my mother. Add to that the only girl in the neighborhood being a little kooky and there is no question you gravitate toward the fun. The men of the house and neighborhood were more interesting, their activities more fun.

It was a long time before I understood what it was like to have a sister. And even longer before I got how special it was. My primary relationship with my Man wasn't working, so the natural bond of my girlfriends became a safe place and one I embraced during the rough times. I remember a lunch discussion where it was agreed our men couldn't fill every role that we needed from them, and that was okay.

My sisters have helped me through and taught me so much; they stood strong for me when I wasn't able to. They filled in gaps when I didn't have the courage to even get out of bed. They taught me to lead with my heart. By some indefinable sisterhood of solace and understanding, our hearts breathed together. They weren't my sisters by blood but my sisters by choice. To paraphrase the title song from Mame. "They made me feel alive again, gave me the drive again." Nothing like an estrogen filled rally where the combined wisdom answers questions and definitively supports the tribe.

I reprint part of an email I sent to my girlfriends after the split, in response to a dear friend sending me one of those chain e-mails celebrating girlfriends.

> *Sisterhood is forged not so much by time but through*
> *understanding and with that, your compassion, friendship,*
> *laughter, tears, invitations, insights and beautiful spirits*
> *I have been taught so much.*

There hasn't been a day that I've not thought about, reached
out for and needed the understanding that has come from the
women in my life.

I've been on this journey to figure out where I fit in the
world, who I am as a woman and who I want to be as a human
being. The days bring all kinds of insights and while it will
be a never ending quest, I know you all will be with me no
matter what, and that has given me a strength I didn't know I
had. I love you guys and even though we were not born sisters,
I couldn't have asked for a better sister family.

We are in a time where we have lost our sense of humanity.
Globalization has widened our viewpoint but has not increased
our connectedness. Instead, barriers have been established,
freedoms have been undermined and blinders have grown
and grown. Rabbit holes have sprung up along the way and
millions have segmented into these holes.

Within this framework, my sister family, whose experience
brought me wisdom, whose intelligence and caring taught
me kindness, whose presence stood with me, and whose
spirits understand my journey, keep me strong. Connecting,
coinciding, collaborating, eventually helping me heal.

I have my sister friends. Lucky me.

Lost & Found

I was afraid. I was afraid I would die again. I had leapt off the cliff to end my relationship, and I would need to do it again and probably again.

I was afraid to speak as though it were my life I was living. I was afraid to live my life outside of the judgemental obervationalist I had become. I was afraid if people really knew me, they wouldn't like me. I was afraid to lose anymore friends. I had set up an invisible bodyguard determined to protect me. This bodyguard distorted everything, clouded the connectors, questioned my perceptions, muffled my intuition and misdirected my mojo.

> *It was once*
> *Then not again*
> *My hopes at finding such*
> *Lies within*
> *Never once and never more*
> *Does one so sweet*
> *And sorrowful soar*

Lights started to flicker in the distance. I saw something. It resonated. It didn't last long enough to be recognized and then it faded. I wouldn't let it go. I looked closer.

A flash. A moment. Your heart knows.

My way of being in the world was flawed. Long ago I had lost touch with my inner everything. I would need to reclaim it.

I knew how far I would need to go to reclaim my voice. I knew it wasn't going to be pleasant, but I also knew, I could do it. It was me, after all. The grief and the growth and the grasping would be good things.

Johann Wolfgang Goethe said it best.

> *And so long as you haven't experienced this*
> *to die and so to grow,*
> *you are only a troubled guest*
> *on the dark earth.*

I didn't want to be a troubled guest anymore. I could die and grow like the best of them. I could redo myself. I could find a way to listen to my heart's symphony, to hear that faraway aria through the distracting cries. I'll meet myself on the other side of this new death. I could practice another way of being in the world.

What was lost could be found. David Whyte hit it hard.

> *The day I saw beneath dark clouds*
> *the passing light over the water*
> *and I heard the voice of the world speak out,*
> *I knew then, life is no passing memory of what has been*
> *nor the remaining pages in a great book waiting to be read.*

It is the opening of eyes long closed.
It is the vision of far off things
seen for the silence they hold.
It is the heart after years
of secret conversing
speaking out loud in the clear air.

I listened as if my life depended on it.

My story is happiness. My story is intellectual conversations. My story is creativity, compassion, integrity.

It is okay to ask for what you want.

I am strong. I am purposeful.

I love who I am and where I am.

I have all the patience for the great things that await me.

It is okay to need help.

It is okay to ask for that help.

I can listen and trust and speak from my heart. I can stand up for myself. I can get through tough situations. I can confront people emotionally. I won't hate myself. I won't feel terrible. I will be okay if I disagree with someone. I will not lose friends or favor if I let people know the truth. And if I lose them, good riddance. I am safe.

Hearing new thoughts replacing old thoughts, "Speaking out loud into the clear air," spending time in care and feeding the new me, I began to believe I was more than my judgements. I saw the change in how I felt. I saw what was feeding me and what wasn't. I felt who was feeding me. I heard my thoughts and listened to them. I understood the difference between forcing myself to change how I felt, and just being. I felt things and people speaking to me, and I moved towards those elements that brought me more and more into being. Then, wrapped in my new being, I embraced feelings of belonging. I embraced the sounds of support.

This belonging pushed me through the many falsehoods helping me find what was there all along. The open channel to my heart. That indefinable and indescribable existence of my soul's code. All this part of the magic, part of the mania free endeavors, part of the mystery that fueled the new Mel.

I grow. I go. I do. I'm hurt; it's okay. I assess. I try again. I take three steps forward and five back and now know it is cool. The lost connection has been identified. The fever associated with finding it no longer flaming. The protector no longer on guard.

I'm not stuck under the tyranny. I'm not stuck in the muck of not understanding. I'm not the lost little kid who didn't understand and kept trying. I found my voice by quieting the crazies or as my friend calls them, the gremlins.

Kander and Ebb said it with feeling. "Now I am calm, safe and serene, heartache and hurt are no longer a part of the scene. Isn't it better, the way it should be."

If you worry about what other people think, if you listen to your untruths, you lose touch with the truest part of yourself. Quieting the worry allowed other sounds and beats and feelings and truths to be heard.

Long ago I had lost touch with that inner drummer, that inner helper, that inner Mel. As I listened and heard that inner self, I helped strengthen its voice with practice. Day by day it grows louder and stronger and feels more and more freedom to sing. Found and lost. Lost and found. Me (speaking into the clear air) at last.

Contentment

I love my tree house where I live because it is mine. I love my tree house because I thought and thought and pictured the perfect place to write and grow and recover and it appeared. I love my bed because I sweated over buying it and made the decision to spend way more than I could afford so it was right. I love my bed because I asked for help and it was graciously given. I love my bed because every night I go to sleep and know I made a choice to be content.

When I moved into my tree house, I spent what money I had on a bed and a television. I didn't need anything else. I would acquire pieces as time and finances dictated. I would add things to my life that I picked out, that spoke to me, that gave me a sense of peace. Anything I wanted would wait until I took care of the things that I needed, things that would feed me. Things that would feed the me I was becoming. Time and patience would reveal what was right. Piece by piece I was putting it together. "It goes like it goes, like a river it flows" and who was I to move or act against the flow? I no longer had any ego attached to the challenge of redirecting it; I would step into the flow. Put the Mel ship in the water and move on and in.

I marvelled at the power of making this choice and how that one decision fueled me, accelerating me into inescapable realizations.

I love the kindnesses, the accomplishments, the people who came into my life, the jobs, the experiences, all part of a life affirming chain of being and letting myself flow into creation. An oh so interconnected existence. Integrated and special and perfect.

In the words of Stephen Schwartz, "If I'm not tied to anything, I'll never be free."

Here's to being tied down!

The perfect comforter appeared. I rushed out to purchase it at the local Pottery Barn only to get there and be told they don't carry comforters - that is internet only. Okay. I shopped the clearance section and found two perfect condiment trays for the party I would have when the time was right. As the manager was ringing up the dishes, I had a hunch and asked her about the comforter. It was in the backroom. Odd that a floor salesperson would say they didn't have it. Viola. Success. I love my comforter because every night it covers me, warms me in support, protecting my sleeping, dreaming self. I love my vacuum cleaner. I love my vacuum cleaner because it was a gift and it does an amazing job. I am filled with joy when it cleans the carpet, bringing my tree house to a gleaming perfection.

If I had patience and followed my instincts and didn't listen to goofy Mel chatter, then things not only could materialize, they would.

Staying in the flow wasn't without its challenges. Old patterns die hard. I would take three steps forward and six back. The bad news. Going backward sucks. The good news. I had experienced those steps forward; I had held them and felt them and even if I was in a pit of despair at losing ground, I knew I could get there again.

In one moment of pushing and not flowing, I'll admit it, I lost faith. The perfect desk didn't appear, and I needed one so badly. I forced the pace. I purchased an out of stock desk that can only be described as a monstrosity. When I went to pick it up it was so large, I could barely get it in the truck, and it was so not right, people I didn't know were shaking their heads in apparent disgust. It would never fit into my office, let alone my tree house and certainly not my life. I did a U-turn, returned it, vowing to wait for the right thing to fall into my lap and it did...

I love my desk because it was made for me. I sit and write and dream at this desk. I'm inspired and excited about everything from this desk. When my desk was installed the universe brought me the perfect task chair. The night I put my laptop on my new desk and began to work propped up on a broken folding chair. I did an internet search on Craigslist. Viola. A 1965 Charles Pollack, Knoll Manufactured blue velvet executive task chair. So fabulous, so perfect. As luck would have it, just moments before I did my search, a fellow writer had posted the chair. It was way more than I wanted to spend, way more than I've ever spent on a desk chair, but it spoke to me, it called my name, it screamed, "Buy me!" When I was ready to get serious about my writing future, there it was, waiting for my call, to come to my rescue and give me a perfect place to sit to do my work.

When you are open and free from the chaos of daily existence and the to dos, when you can find a place as William Blake said, "Where Satan can not find you," everything is there waiting. You just have to be willing to pull off the blinders and breathe. Everything had something to say to me once I made my choice to be the best Mel I could be. I opened up and let it all in, even though it was scary as shit.

I love my kitchen that is just small enough to be perfect. I love my kitchen because I can only fit a coffee maker comfortably on my counter. I love my kitchen because it forced me to put my microwave in the closet. I love my microwave that resides in my closet. It is a treat to go into the closet and toss some microwaveable item or to reheat a dish and emerge from the closet with a tasty morsel that feeds me. I love my bowls that I waited and waited to find. For months I had eaten cereal, Spaghettios, you name it, out of a crystal nut bowl from the Princess House Crystal Collection. The only use this bowl ever got in its 30 year life. I now have four perfect white bowls. They sit in an exposed pantry displaying beautifully my four plates, two serving trays, two platters and two condiment trays. This area of my tree house is a testament to patience and waiting for the right choices to unfold. I love my chocolate ceramic matching lamps that called my name when I walked by them at the Restoration Hardware outlet store. They needed to be part of the lighting scheme for my home, and they let me know it.

Not only did they let me know it, the salesperson, an oversized manager of the stock room, walked me through selecting the right shade, he ran into the backroom, bringing out different lampshades and presented me with design options and helped cement the perfection that was making a nourishing choice to cast light on my new home.

I love my little brother. I love my little brother for handing me a chilled shot of tequila when I was laid out flat on my back in his guest room unable to move from the pain in my lower back. I love my little brother for saying, "It can't hurt." I love my best friend who became my best girl after one long, disastrous, accident filled day. Who laughed with me when the hot emergency room doctor gave me the thumbs up, then she became my emergency contact on the checkout forms and shook her head enthusiastically when the late night billing checkout woman asked if she was "My best girl." Then she drove me home, stopped for a Taco Bell burrito, delivered me into bed and watched an hour of reality television with me before heading back to her fiance. I love my therapist, referred to me by one of my kookier but fabulous friends. I love my therapist because every meeting affirms the choice I made toward a better me. I love my therapist because she holds everything I say and mentors me through my confusion and helps me hear the truth. I love my therapist because she helped me untangle the past and horizons the future for me. If everyone went to someone like her, the world would be a better place.

Most importantly, I love the friends that are with me still and the new friends I made as the new Mel emerged. I love the calls, the feeling, the laughter and the joy of putting myself in another's eyes and feeling held and understood. I love the friends who dumped me, who couldn't be bothered, who didn't want to get caught in the muck of the sinking Mel ship. I love these friends, because they made the relationships I do have sing a magnificent tune.

There is no nobler pursuit than that of your dreams, and I love how lucky I am to be able to pursue my dreams wholeheartedly. I love how I can celebrate all that I have and appreciate all the ways they have made me who I am.

So many people have helped me in my life. One of my favorite things on the old Mel path had been the deep knowledge that I could always "count on the kindness of strangers." How strange and wonderful at last to have the wild realization that you can rely on loved ones as well. I love the way receiving support was more and more effortless the freer I became from my shameful past belief that help was a hindrance and something to be avoided at all costs.

> *How much happier would I be*
> *If I knew the secrets of the tree*
> *If I let myself be*
> *What a wondrous thing for me*
> *Never to have a doubt*
> *Never to have a care*
> *If I let myself be*
> *the tree.*

I love things now that are effortless. That I don't need to struggle, and mangle, and manhandle and force into existence. I love that I can just be.

Overachieving

There I was overachieving, crossing things off my list, over helping, over analyzing, figuring I could make everything right for everyone I ran into. It didn't matter how long I knew the person, I could absorb anyone's problem in record time and my ego assured me I could make everything right. "Right" for me meant that I would be good enough.

My first block lettered writings in my first ruled notebook was a list of things I needed to achieve before I could be happy. As I learned, the list grew. As I grew, the list grew. As I achieved, the list grew. I added fears to my list, telling myself, if I was afraid I must face it. I added adventures to my list. I added everything to my list. It was never ending.

I had no idea I had set myself up to fail.

Each success pushed me further into a state I couldn't label and had no way of understanding. The more success I had, the larger the pit of anxiety and despair. I remember crying for no reason after meetings, after screenings, after closings, after conversations. I remember feeling terrible after achieving my goals. I remember saying to myself, I guess I have to set higher goals. Challenge myself more. I feel like crap. It must be that I didn't test myself enough. I needed bigger obstacles, higher mountains to climb. That was the answer. The bigger the challenge, the better. The more varied the tasks I set up in front of myself to be tackled and vanquished, the more impossibilities erased, I might win some pardon from judgement row.

There are many reasons to have a never ending list of things to do; it keeps you from thinking; it keeps up a treadmill of activity that you can never fulfill; but mostly, it helps you keep track of your insanity.

My list included everything from the life changing, to the fear defying, to the mundane.

One rainy Halloween week the opportunity to face a long time fear of dressing up in a costume and going to a party presented itself.

You'd think hiding behind a mask would be something I would embrace and be comfortable with. Not the case. Since everything about my sense of well being was already a convoluted cover adding a costume only threatened to tip the balance of sanity beyond my control.

From the minute I committed to attending the Halloween party, I was on the super edge. I was on Torture Lane. I shopped costume places; I sweated over ideas; I chatted with friends and couldn't settle on anything. I didn't want to go sexy, couldn't figure out clever, and ironic is so hard to pull off and can go horribly awry. I didn't want to be a superhero, because, let's be honest. That's just lame. The party was fast approaching, and I had nothing but my fear and my terror and one last shot to pull off a costume before I would have to cancel and accept defeat. One of my friends had a collection of paraphernalia from characters she's created in her many years of doing improv. She let it be known I was more than welcome to go and select anything that might help. She had props, outfits, costumes, clothes, shoes and wigs. I made the most of her collection, not really choosing anything specific, but picking pieces that were comfortable, stylish and twisted. My props included a grey haired wig, a pill box hat, silver cat eye glasses, a granny handbag, white hand gloves and a heavy silk print dress. I envisioned a kind of Mel in disguise, like I was going undercover a la Peter Sellers in The Pink Panther series of films.

"What are you... Mrs. Doubtfire?" was one of the first things I heard on entering the party. Grabbing a Margarita rocks, no salt, "Hey, funny, Church Lady!' Taking some pictures with a satanic skeleton who was scratching out the music, "You look like my Aunt Mable."

By the end of the party my fear had subsided; my terror was gone. I made it through the night, had some laughs, had some realizations and when twelve teenagers hanging out at a Del Taco yelled, "Hey old lady, nice ass!" I remembered I had a good time.

As I crossed "Ridiculous Fear of Dressing Up" off my list, I questioned the whole damn thing. There were so many things that I appreciated about having a list of things to do. The problem was my self esteem never rose to meet my accomplishments, and no matter what I did I never felt good enough. Perhaps it was time to let go of my list.

Life

When your name rhymes with klutz and when you can add almost any consonant to form a fun pun: slutz, tutz, putz, nutz, it's a recipe for a self deprecating life.

In the third grade Fall Spectacular, I was cast with a particularly large classmate named Charlotte. Charlotte and I were to play Siamese twins, two parts of one oversized dress. We were to have a fight, split up, the dress would rip and we walk off the stage in different directions. Dress rehearsals went fine. During the big performance, we hit our lines perfectly, and when we went for the split, unfortunately for me, the dress ripped only part way, stopping at the double hem we had not cut completely through. Being the lighter of the duo, I boomeranged on the snag, bounced off Charlotte, and landed on the ground in a thud. The entire auditorium erupted in laughter. Embarrassed. Sure. Did I get a laugh. Definitely. Funny Girl. I wasn't. It was an accident.

I always considered myself klutzy, clumsy, accident prone, awkward, bumbling, you name it. I learned to embrace all of it. Bounce off the chubby girl, get the laugh. Who cares how it was supposed to go down. Who cares if it didn't work the way it was planned. You can get a laugh either way. Some type of "spin" factor became second nature. I could accept my kluzty way of being and control any "accident" to come.

My strategy was simple. Go for the laugh first. If I had some deficiency, I would easily make that deficiency my shield of armor. I would make a joke. Laugh and the world laughs with you. How self satisfying and seductive to reach for the self deprecating zinger based on analyzing a situation and pumping out the perfect words before anyone had the chance to feel or comment or blink.

> *we travel so well*
> *we work at a pace*
> *we play for a message*
> *we laugh with our cake*
> *we cry over fate*
> *when it's all perfect*
> *and nothings not wrong*
> *then you'll have found*
> *it was you all along.*

I heard myself explaining how I was lucky that I learned how to take falls from my years playing soccer, saving my klutzy self from ever getting seriously hurt. I learned how to roll with a fall. Give over to the accident, let go and lean into it. An inspired individual who heard this told me I wasn't klutzy, suggested I stop saying I'm klutzy, that accidents happen and instead of beating my psyche up, take the lesson of leaning into a fall.

I couldn't believe what I had just heard. I couldn't believe that I could stop calling myself klutzy, let alone turn a "beat down" belief into a positive.

Everything came back to moving toward the element in which I belonged. What I defined as the "humor defense," the "klutz instinct" closed off the true joy of ascending through the imperfections that made me perfectly Mel.

No more questing, no more beat down, no more calling myself a klutz. Klutzy - just another state of mind to be faced and defeated.

Whatever circumstance, whatever situation you find yourself. The choice of accepting your awkward way of being, the choice of making a life's work of you and no one else was critical. I owed myself the opportunity to make living my life, my life's work. My way. Find it. Live it. Do it. Embrace it. Don't stop trying. Don't stop pushing. Go for it. Make a choice that everything is part of the larger picture that is wonderfully you.

I stopped and did the brave thing, revealed myself.

Fat and Gross

It's a no brainer. I stink. I'm no good. I am fat and gross. Darn. It's even easy to type. It was like a protective armor. If I told myself I was fat and gross, anything anyone said about me would be a step up. If I told myself I was fat and gross, I wouldn't make heinous fashion choices that could draw attention to myself. If I told myself I was fat and gross, no one could hurt me. I was riding the bench of reversed expressionism. Calculated, choreographed and flawed. Blending was the way to go. You couldn't get in trouble or be embarrassed or be in any kind of pain as long as you hid how fat and gross you were and fit in.

Fitting in for me, involved having items that made you cool enough to participate but not be thought unhip. Nothing showy or over the top. No drawing attention. Blend at all costs.

All of this fat and gross business was a flogging of the very foundation of sense and sensibility. It was a pattern I could not stop. I loved how I defeated one pattern and another pattern sprang up in its place. It's not the thing you fear but the mother of the thing you fear.

By continually feeding myself falsehoods and trash talking I grew fat and gross on the inside. I ate from my own slanders, and it was the worst diet I've ever been on. These fatty word deposits became an active growing account with no end in sight. My appetite for bad talking myself was voracious. If I was fat and gross, I just needed to accept the fact that I was fat, gross and disgusting and love my fat, gross and disgusting self. But, if I wasn't fat, gross and disgusting, I would have to stop labeling myself.

Something cried out. Enough. Enough. I wasn't fat and gross. I wasn't hideous. I wasn't the story I was telling myself.

Any journey needs to begin somewhere, that first step, and while it does not need to have a destination, it most certainly is a journey.

A moment of clarity? A moment of inspiration? I needed to step into my fear and come out with the truth. What it was, I didn't know. I hoped it would be. Who cares how I look and what my body was like, it wasn't what made me the person I wanted to be. It wasn't the beginning or ending of what I could be. There had to be a place where I didn't care and it didn't matter how I looked, just that I was happy. Content. Fulfilled. A marriage of the inner and outer me.

I wasn't ready to bounce around the swimming pool playing Marco Polo and drinking Coronas in a bikini, but I was ready to take my coat off and dance. And dance I did. Fat and gross could be a thing of the past. Not of the future.

A Self Portrait

Many artists have explored self portraits; to me, all of them are interesting. A self portrait can reveal anything and everything. Focus, spirituality, individuality, distrust, happiness, selfness, introspection, exploration, intimidation.

I love the many self portraits I have seen, read or listened to through the years. Diane Arbus, Rembrandt, Picasso, Van Gogh, David Whyte, Bob Dylan, Frida Kahlo, just to name a few.

I was influenced at an early age by the idea of life "through a looking glass." Photography has always been a huge part of my life. Two weeks away from my own wedding day, the sun was setting on the private swanky beach club hosting a friend's wedding reception. I slipped away from the celebration to enjoy some sunset alone time. Feeling not too disgusting, I decided to turn the digital camera on myself and snapped a self portrait. As the sun disappeared, I threw my digital camera in my bag and rejoined the celebration.

Months passed and the bloom of my marriage had crashed around me. I was licking my wounds in the Lobster Room, cleaning out my digital photo collection. The last thing you need in a stressful time is to be reminded over and over again of the moments spent with friends and the Ex. As I got rid of event after event, I caught sight of the self portrait from my friend's wedding and clicked on the picture I had taken of myself with that gorgeous sunset in October. Memories flooded back to the time when I had stepped away from the wedding for some Mel time. My first thought about "the photo" staring back at me was horrific. I looked hideous. I couldn't look at it. I couldn't accept that was how I looked. I couldn't accept that was me.

For some reason, I was unable to delete that picture. I moved it to my desktop. I had taken some hard steps and still I said these horrible things about myself. Enough.

There's a great lyric by Edward Kleban from A Chorus Line that makes the statement in its own way.

> *Who am I anyway?*
> *Am I my resume?*
> *An 8x10 picture*
> *of a person I don't know.*

Every moment dissected, showcased, a distortion ever playing, ever to be measured up to, ever to be measured against. A false picture I could never equal. Perfection's humor had painted a lovely portrait that stood proudly in the foyer hanging across the entry way to my life. My own portrait of Anxiety Gray. A joke played from childhood. A laugh I forgot to have.

I wanted to know who I was and what that meant.

Am I trying to manipulate?

Am I trying to deviate?

Am I trying to damage?

Am I going to be okay?

This sucks.

My false self portrait ever tipping toward an eve of some horrible destruction. Always there, never closing down for business.

I was so clouded in twisted stories and complicated, renderings my only choice was to do the scariest thing of all, accept the image that stared back at me.

Face my fear. I pulled the digital shot into Photoshop and went to work. I played with this moment in time. I used filters and the essence of my self portrait came into clarity. I edged into the light and shadows, the pain and the purpose, and illuminated the picture, with all my flaws and perfections.

The final image emerged.

It needed one more touch. I created a mini LUTZ logo and popped it in the corner of the self portrait, like a tiny little signature. I had branded my self portrait.

Something liberating began to pulse in the air. Stately, stylish and a breed apart. I saw a confidence I didn't feel. I saw the art in the madness. I saw something staring back at me.

I decided I would need to wear my brand, my image, my self portrait and own it. I would have to expose that which I hated for all to see until the time that I could accept the image that reflected back at me. It was a moment I remember clearly. I had found some T-shirts in the 3 for 5 dollar rack at American Apparel. They were brown with a purple ring around the collar and sleeves. A Swedish designer I loved used to iron-on his designs to T-shirts. It seemed simple. I had an iron. I bought some iron-on paper and steamed the abhorred image of Mel, my created self portrait, onto a T-shirt.

I wore that T-shirt as a symbol of acceptance. I wore that perceived hideous picture of myself as a statement, and felt an embrace I had never known.

The Mel Shirt was born.

To my surprise, the image was greeted with great warmth. People even wanted, clamored is the best word, to have their own Mel Shirt. Something was clear to me. I wasn't as hideous as I thought. There was more going on here than just a picture.

By branding myself, I had faced one of the toughest patterns of my life. The imagined ugliness began melting away. I was directing a changeover. I was coming to terms with who I am. An ember, asked for and prayed for, had caught fire, and I was coaxing the fire into a blaze of being.

The Mel Shirt was the first step on a road that I travel every day. A road of great acceptance of myself and others, a road that has no end. A road I can travel safe in the knowledge that I can take the ups and downs, twists and turns and accept the whole picture. I would wear my Mel Shirt on days that I needed that extra comfort, the extra nourishment that would only come from embracing the new me. The Mel that was forming on a positive foundation of self acceptance. The Mel

Shirt became that little extra hug of support that I needed.

My self portrait happened of its own will. Unexpectedly my personal snap shot revealed tons. It was a final key to the locked personal puzzle. A key that allowed me to untangle and supplant my mania.

I manufactured a self portrait, and it became a tool that helped me. The individuality of this step toward self understanding laid bare a truth.

Your picture of yourself is not how others see you. I was not what I had been telling myself.

Enough

If only I was good enough everything would be okay. For what, I didn't know. Enough. Enough. Enough. There was always some reason to feel not good enough.

I reprint an e-mail I sent to my therapist.

It is hard for me to change from the belief or coding or programming that if only I was cooler, smarter, whatever... that things would work out and I'd be okay. It's a quirky control thing. I'm also disappointed in myself. I can't seem to shake the idea that I'm not good enough and I need to try harder. I guess that is part of the above.

I appreciate you letting me process through this. It is a tough one to get through and I seem to be spinning and trying (not succeeding) to focus on grounding myself. The pain makes it harder on all fronts.

Happy Monday! And thanks again!

Ps. I love how I always end on an up note. I like to be

positive when I am freaking out.

My therapist responded quickly and decisively.

*The fear that we are not enough is indeed a tough one. It is
only that - a fear - not the truth.*
*Whenever you find yourself wanting to explain yourself more,
keep reminding yourself that you are enough - more than
enough. Even if you don't believe it at first, you will
believe it eventually.*
*There is a pattern of perfection at the center of your being
which has never been touched by disease, misfortune, feelings
of not being enough, etc. etc. - Keep breathing into that
place, and keep affirming that place.*

Enough. More than enough. Was she high? What would I
do if I didn't explain myself more? Was I really enough?

"Keep breathing into that place..." What place? Was it
somewhere in New Jersey?

Don't get distracted. Don't get side tracked. Don't let your
anxiety and fear run you off the course. She said to breathe
into it. There it was in black and white. I was good enough.
Could I believe it? I had to. My conscious self having been told
I was enough, having been shown the picture of who I could
be, ran around like a chicken with its head cut off, looking for
any comfort, any port in a storm. Breathing became my only
outlet to stop the chicken. Grounding was something I would
need to learn. Breathe.

Ground yourself in the truth. Simple. Perfect. Breathe. In-
tellectually I understood the problem, but my patterned mind
and body were playing catch up. It had been many years of

telling myself I wasn't good enough.

Back to Sondheim. "Stop worrying where you're going. Move on. If you can know where you are going, you've gone. Just keep moving on." Know you are good enough and move on. Breathe.

You know when something is right. When it has been performed so precisely enmeshing with the individual making the presentation. You can feel the truth oozing from every pore. That is why great art evokes awe and inspiration and exploration. Others can imitate the work, even do it in such a way that it explodes with their truth. Different, perhaps, but a truth is a truth. You can measure much in the tune or the vibration that resonates from the source. When not performed via a conduit of truth the work rings false. We can relate to a soul searing rendition, a belting of the truth, because we can all connect with that universal energy. Once the truth has been spoken, anything untrue, or short of the beauty of truth, rings false.

The more I believed I was good enough, the easier to call out on the mat the patter that kept telling me I wasn't enough. The more I practiced telling myself I was okay and enough, the freer I became and the less I felt I would be destroyed for not making the grade.

Once you've committed to being enough, there is no going back; your very being doesn't allow it. You can only bask in the place you are going. No pale imitation of some grander truth allowed. Just your truth in all its blinding light. This is the coolest thing about getting to a place where you are breathing into the truth. Your body doesn't let you do anything to screw up the feeding, and the breathing cements the bricks of truth. It lets you know when you clunk a bad note and aren't on the right path. The breathing works to shake you, disturb you, anchor you, and organize you. It helps create harmony.

"I chose and my world was shaken. so what, the choice may have been mistaken, the choosing was not, you have to move on."

Moving on to me now meant breathing into the choices I had made to be a better me. It meant breathing into that place where I was safe and more than enough. It meant believing.

"Look at what you want, not at where you are, not at what you'll be. Look at the things you've done for me. Opened up my eyes, taught me how to see." The penultimate moment from Sondheim's Sunday in the Park with George, lovingly sung by Bernadette Peters.

Breathing is a glorious grounder. It is something that feeds us; it can be interpreted and integrated and can be a practice. Any way you slice it, your breath is a part of you.

I tied my breathing to statements that would nourish me. I practiced those statements. I started with obvious ones, dumb ones, universal ones, empowering ones, funny ones, anything that would reverse what I deemed as negative and self destructive thoughts. It was amazing what years of mania could create. What stories whispered to your conscious and subconscious mind that you believed in so deeply as to not question them. I was so happy to know I wasn't my past. I wasn't the twisted tales I had been feeding myself. It was just a matter of flipping that switch, standing in the light, breathing through to the other side and finally buying into the idea that my fear of not being enough wasn't the truth.

Advice

The grounded self can accept comments, can understand the context in which advice is offered, can even establish the necessary boundaries to take the words in. A centered self can respond, react, evaluate and utilize input. The crazed self has no business even trying.

In my fractured state of being, I craved advice, desperately. Perhaps someone had the answer to my burning pain. Maybe this turn of phrase would bring me to the place of truth that I so desired.

Every piece of advice given, I listened to; if someone was taking the time to offer it, perhaps it was something I needed to hear. I couldn't stop people from giving me advice, and I couldn't stop myself from asking for it.

Some of my favorites...

"When in doubt do nothing." Do nothing. Quite possibly the most difficult thing I could master.

A particular favorite of mine: "Burn everything."

"Make a list of positive things about yourself." (I could never think of one.)

"Take a look at the monkeys. Their smiles will help." (Huh?)

"Develop a hobby." (like ice fishing?)

My attorney's favorite **acronym**... "N.M.F.P." (Not My F@#!@N Problem)

I quite liked this one; "In order to find yourself, you must lose yourself." (If only I could lose myself.)

"Look at events as bridges not barriers." (Plato calling)

"Start traditions in the life you are in, that will reflect your hopes for the life you want." (Buddha anyone?)

"Just stand when there's nothing left to do." (The bible according to Oprah)

After all of these lovely advice gems, a strange thing happened, I would hear myself giving advice to others that I needed to hear.

"It's time to start taking care of yourself. You can help all of these people after you've taken care of yourself and your business. Everyone can handle their own shit. Let them."

Cole Porter popped, "Is it a cocktail, this feeling of joy? Or is what I feel the real mccoy?"

What is essential is invisible to the eye. Keep working on the inner world, the inner Mel. Stay the course and don't get distracted. Take care of self, find a way to feel safe and confident. Don't worry about others.

I took my own advice.

Support

I didn't understand the concept of support. I had never really allowed myself to let a nourishing relationship unfold. I didn't know how it felt to be supported. I certainly never allowed myself to enjoy support. I didn't know what it meant or how to react to support and not crumble into dust. I was dealing with a tremendous deficit in this support arena and my ocean of need so great I was fearful any support would wipe me out. I've always been there as a support player for others in a way that got twisted. Much easier to give than to receive.

For years, the support I received felt painful. Like a knife stabbing me in the stomach. I would go to painstaking efforts to avoid getting any help or support. I would devise terrific schemes so as not to need a ride, have someone help me move, you name it. I toiled on my own. The mere thought of asking someone for something was never comfortable. Asking strangers for help was easier, but the closer I got to someone, the more terror in asking for their help. And, if I did ask some-one for something and they couldn't do it: It was a horror. I would berate myself for days after asking someone to pick me up. Luckily, the old Mel who accepted this type of behavior was disappearing. The new emerging Mel saw the light of ac-cepting support as a natural part of being human. Support was a good thing. I needed to learn to accept support and not get tripped up or lost or weirded out. Practice the perfection and art of receiving support.

> *a tear fell*
> *a deep well of forgiveness*
> *a laughing twist of fate*
> *a tear fell*
> *and the drone continued*
> *the distance deepened*
> *and the twine grew*
> *a tear fell*
> *and all that was hoped for came through*
> *without sorrow without sadness*
> *all was revealed*
> *a tear fell*
> *and said it all*
> *the devastation and distraction*
> *the pain and the purpose*
> *the fall and the rise*
> *a tear fell*

At desperate moments, where I felt the most alone and

vulnerable, the universe met me with dazzling surprise angels wrapped in many packages. Packages of hot mechanics, friends calling at the right moment, gallant strangers, a retired doctor, my gynecologist, renowned authors. Heroes, one and all. "Is everything okay?" came from my best friend when I had called her cell phone in a desperate fear induced reach out only to not leave a message when she didn't answer.

"I'm here to help." The hottest tire store worker you can imagine when my tire blew out in LA Friday traffic and the tow company put me on their pay no mind list.

"It's going to be okay" a hunky trainer that I started working out with to help me through some lower back problems and with whom I could only cry when confronted by the pain during our workout time together. He helped me get through the workouts. He worked with me and guided me to work through the pain. He supported me during stretches and exercises and pushed me further than I would have gone on my own. I learned a lot from him, and while I didn't continue on with him as my personal trainer, I took the lesson. We all need help to get through.

It was such an amazing thing to experience how people pushed past my defenses, looked beyond my polite refusals and jumped the fence to reach me. As I was met, I would consciously bite my tongue and avoid the comfortable, "No, I don't need anything." Of course I needed help; it was obvious, just say yes. Everyone needs help. I had to do whatever it took to stop my fear and quit rejecting help. Luckily once I stopped out of hand rejecting help, I could force myself to ask for help when I needed it. In the beginning, it was like calling up the hottest boy in school and asking him out on a date. I was nervous as a mofo every time I asked for help. It got easier and easier the more I practiced.

These magical people came into my life and showed me the way. I am grateful for the many lessons I was taught.

I still have moments of panic when I ask for or accept help. But I just keep jumping into the deep end of the support pool, and each time I am met, each time a life raft is thrown out to rescue me from my folly. I get stronger. These inspired individuals provided the necessary brush strokes to color in the Mel picture. Brush stroke after brush stroke of kindness and support created a depth of field that could withstand my ocean of need. Giving and receiving coming into balance. I was no longer adrift. By accepting support, I had gone the longest way toward accepting myself.

Love

I hadn't learned how to love someone and still take care of me. Love. Tormented and twisted and so foreign. Love. It came and went so illusively. I couldn't get a beat on what was true about love. Love for me was a never ending proof of worthiness. If I performed correctly, I would be rewarded with love. If I acted correctly, love was waiting around the corner. I was used to people who loved me, belittling, berating and generally not being kind to me. My favorite example was when my mother, upon arrival at my new home in Beverly Hills got out of her car and busted out with a confidence building, "Are you crazy?" This was the first thing out of her mouth. It didn't matter what she meant. My defenses were always up; I was on guard with anyone and everyone entering my life.

All I knew of love was how to live without it.

There's no question my existence played itself out in two parts. Love of others and love of self.

Love of others.

I know why I've been able to help so many people and not be able to help myself. Where was it written in the Mel playbook that it wasn't important to have the people closest to you be supportive. I was longing for love and support so badly I would do anything to get it. I recognized in other people their need to be loved and accepted. I exhausted myself working to make people feel okay, then in turn I would finally be rewarded with being okay and worthy of love.

My Ex Man used to say it was an amazing feeling to be loved by me. In return, he loved me in the way he could. The fact that it was self centered, conditional and awash in anxiety and insecurity, I never understood. One of his favorite statements to me was how easy I was to love. I never got the translation, "It is so great that you only serve my needs and don't demand or need anything." I never felt awash in love or comforted, or supported, or safe, just the familiar feeling to my relationship with my family. It was familiar. If I was better, did more, tried harder, I would be worthy of the kind of love I craved and would be okay. It was me. I wasn't good enough to be loved. I had set land mines around me, detonating if things ever got too close. Protecting myself from the truest form of being loved. It wasn't anyone's fault. No one was to blame. I just had no idea how to ask for what I wanted. It was a big blank screen inside of me.

I would be lying if I led you to believe I never let my guard down. My guard came way down only to bring a glimpse of what could be, a picture appeared on the screen, followed by the terror and the retreat back into my tower of shame. My defenses kept me blind to the pain and uncertainty of my constant craving for love and acceptance. I so badly wanted to feel right. But the path I chose left me standing outside the door.

It became quite clear to me one holiday. I had been invited over for the obligatory Thanksgiving family gathering. I showed up at the appointed hour with my expectations sufficiently in place. Low. The basement. As I stood outside the door and knocked. No one answered. Time ticked by. I waited. Nothing. I knocked again, a little louder. Nothing. Hmmmm. What was going on? Where was everyone? Finally some movement. The cave door eventually opened revealing one of the inhabitants, my Dad, slightly distressed, and a little groggy. Looking past him around the dimly lit house, devoid of any life, I thought to myself, "Are we going to celebrate the holiday? Am I here at the wrong time?" I squeezed in past the three dogs, wondering what Twilight Zone episode I had entered. My mom was sleeping. My brother was in the bathroom for an extended visit; my brother's wife was reading a magazine, working on her laptop and engrossed in an episode of Law & Order. I scratched my head. I guess all would be revealed. I went to work on cleaning off the cluttered dining room table. I removed the motorcycle helmet, the change, the wallets, the US magazine, the STAR magazine, the long expired prescription medication, the dog bones. I found some candles and made a center piece for the table. When I lit the candles, my brother emerged from his bathroom extravaganza.

Things started to warm up. I moved into the kitchen. Thank God. There was a turkey in the oven. Dinner would be served in 45 minutes. Great.

Knocking on a door where seemingly no one was home, with no warm greeting awaiting me, that was distressed and sleepy and closed, seemed to be a metaphor of my entire existence. I was constantly knocking on a door where no one was home.

One definition of depression that made sense to me "continuing to do the same thing, expecting a different result."

It amazed me that I didn't understand what the disconnect was... The landscape of love forever out of my grasp. Where had I gone wrong? Why did I keep knocking on the same door? Not only that, why did I keep thinking there would be a different outcome?

All I could do was head back to the basics. Who can I love wholeheartedly? Who did I need to love unconditionally? Who can I devote myself to? Who can I vote for? Who could I cheer for? What door could I knock on where someone was always home? Wait. This was an easy one. Mine. Me.

Love of self.

The idea of unconditional love of self had to take root or nothing would. If I wanted this to happen, I'd have to get through the "Like myself" phase, and to do that, took practice. The fun part of divorce and isolation is you are the only person left. Makes things easy.

It took constant talks, affirmations, discussions, you name it, to get on track. Long romantic walks, romantic dinners, indulgent massages, messages to self. This became a hybrid of activities I started to call my Melitation Time. I wasn't the kind of person that meditation came easy to. Instead, I went with what called to me, what I loved to do. I found myself enjoying my Melitation Time. There were many failed but fun attempts as I started to remember what I liked about myself. The relationship grew and blossomed. Amazingly when you start liking yourself, everything starts to change.

"You don't plan to fall in love and when you fall, you fall." Who knew I could fall in love with myself!

What a treat it was to know that unconditional love does exist and that I was capable of providing it for myself. There are so many things I love. People, work, art, personalities, doing the right thing, a fall breeze that's not too cold.

"We'll recall when time runs out, that it only took a moment to be loved a whole life long." Some of my favorite words and music by Jerry Herman puts it into perspective, "Love will come out winning in the closing scene, and when you find it rough contending with the grind that the world puts us through, I can promise you a happy ending."

Once you start loving yourself nothing can get in your way. Take this moment to star in your own show and give yourself a happy ending.

By starting with me. Learning to like myself, loving my oddities, accepting the uniqueness of my way of being. By telling my story fearlessly with no shame, and most importantly free from the terror. When I was able to love myself, I accepted the whole picture and love paraded in from all sources, shining light on areas long thrown into darkness by fear and frustration and lack of understanding.

> *In every tick of the clock*
> *and stroke of the light*
> *Whoever I see and Wherever I go*
> *The timing is perfect*
> *And all is just right.*

My life is now filled with love; it washes over me daily and I live in its promise. Love surrounds me, inspires me and its power has been breaking down barriers and detonating land mines day by day. There is such a thing as unconditional love, and it has no end. Try it on yourself for a full week and see the difference. Pretty cool.

The complicated way I've loved people is gone.

Thank God.

Stop

There are moments when we can be a hero in someone's life. There are moments where we can be a hero in our own life. When you stop worrying. You can do both.

It all became apparent to me. At last.

Stop : to close by filling or obstructing : to hinder or prevent the passage of : to get in the way of : be wounded or killed by

"Having just a vision is no solution, everything depends on execution."

The magic moment had arrived. I was able to stop a thought. When an evil, murderous thought occurred I could notice it and crush it.

Merriam Webster's definition of "stop" goes on and on. To stop contains many pieces of the same puzzle. You have to make a decision. You have to hinder anything that is working against you. I had worked on stopping thoughts, patterns, references, behaviors and still they kept coming at me. Learning to stop worrying was one of the best struggles I've ever been privileged enough to be a part of. One day you know it is under control; the next day you think, "I can do this." I can recognize and stop some thought that isn't serving me. You feel it. You know it, and you are filled with relief.

Stop : to arrest the progress or motion of : cause to halt

You're the only one that can look at what you've done and make the choice you need to make. You have a lot of options. You can beat yourself up with what happened. You can twist around trying to think of what you could have done differently. The nit picking is a choice. A choice you can stop. Now and forever. I'll tell you straight, I kept fighting the idea of stopping. It was easy to see the switch, but something barred me from flipping it to the off position.

It was frustrating to know that I was just a thought away from freedom. That all I needed to do was stop the thoughts. Talking about it helped. I went to the library and got a book on obsessive compulsive behavior called Brain Lock: Free Yourself from Obsessive-Compulsive Behavior by Jeffrey M. Schwartz. It gave me a few tricks on the state of the mind. I had convinced myself that a white knuckle, ball busting effort was all that could be applied.

But why couldn't it be effortless?

Stop : to cause to give up or change a course of action : to keep from carrying out a proposed action

Just change the course of my actions. Easier said than

done. It takes work. It takes practice. Change the course of action away from the pain; let go of the self dislike and get rid of the course map that was so ridiculously created from the anxiety of suffering and the struggle to feel safe. Now's the time. Pull out a blank page. Set a different course. Don't allow yourself to plan on an old map. The heroic thing was making the effort even though it seemed impossible.

Stop : to cause to cease

Cause all actions to cease that don't build toward a healthier destination. Truths rise above the din; moments reveal meaning. This floating of ideas can be noticed and moved aside and becomes the essence of a clear mind. Once you can notice a thought, you can stop it.

I pulled the ripcord to the parachute and stopped the freefall of bad self talk. It was time to begin again.

Stopping freed me. Gave me a power. A switch. Who knew that self torture and personal trash talking could be an addiction and create barriers of entry and distort the relationship with the most important person in your life. The you that you are.

> *In fullness I reached for more*
> *in scarcity I stopped*
> *love without guessing*
> *laugh and say it all*
> *a laugh, a love a life*
> *try for everything*
> *live for it all*

When I stopped, I resisted impulses to label myself. When the fear lived and breathed, bringing back up the bad self talk, I stopped and thought about something life affirming. When the fear of disapproval returned, I stopped and countered with the fear of approval. When the fear of not being enough came up, I stopped and told myself I was more than enough. I couldn't get far enough away to run from the patterns so I stopped and faced them. By noticing and facing them repeatedly, stopping them got easier and easier. Patterns are patterns for a reason. They keep coming at you. You have the power to stop. You have the power to make the choice to stop. To replace anything that isn't serving you. Stop something right now and begin again. This is a very powerful word. A word that is given the command of its intention. Use it. Stop.

Birthdays

There is such a dichotomy in the way that my wants and needs existed and got twisted, my strength and terror tangled and my vision and reality never met. I would want so many things but my method of achieving them was like an elaborate maze or puzzle to reach the prized center. A laughing face over crying eyes was my armor, my existence.

I was capable of not living in distress or discomfort but it became my care taker. It became a terrible companion driving me straight to a collision course with catastrophe. Each event had five pieces; planning, perception, puzzlement, pervasion, and performance. The game was getting people to do what you wanted without giving them a direct clue or telling them what it was you wanted. Picture blindfolding everyone and then getting them to decorate for an elaborate costume party in a great hall you and they had never been to. Imagine living in that blindness but accomplishing perceived perfection anyway. Sound tough? It became second nature. The trial, the struggle, the success. Never easy but always doable. Never quite right but somehow morbidly fun and quite certainly addictive.

My insecurities and self loathing bubbled up around my birthday. I never felt as though anyone would really want to celebrate my birthday, and I was deathly afraid to find out that no one cared about me. I always had a lot of ideas, fueled by my anxieties, so, fun and resentment were always ready to live side by side. I always wanted my birthdays to be perfect. I could never manage a success.

Birthdays became a laughable looking glass for many of my inner struggles.

There was the birthday where I showed up to a dinner party of fifteen men, only two of whom I knew. It was like birthday Mel invited to the Knights of the Roundtable meeting. We got to know each other; we got personal; we had some laughs. The Boys Club Mel Birthday Bash. I still carry affection for some of the men in attendance that night.

There was the birthday where I thought I was going to die. The night before my big day, that I had coordinated, planned, invited 100 people and was catering myself, I came down with an Urinary Tract Infection. I had never had one before and there was no question in my mind, I was never going to see the light of a new day. I imagined John McCain in a POW camp being tortured for years and chided myself into muscling through my birthday evening. Of the hundred people attending, I couldn't think of one person to call to help. It was a hugely successful party. It took me a week to recover.

I laugh at the birthday event thrown by my Best Friend in college. I had a good time. It was the last time we ever spoke. I am still not sure what happened. She apologized to me ten years later.

There was the crab and beer birthday party on the Chesapeake Bay where I slammed my thumb in a sliding glass door. This shooting agony and pain was like a major euphoric drug vibrating through my body, heightening the excitement and the thrill of the party. I had the best time, until for the month that followed, I had to learn how to write and dress with my left hand.

I tried throwing a "drinks and cake" birthday party at a happening night spot where I invited one and all. I drove to the place at the allotted hour, had two drinks on an empty stomach and participated in a birthday round of shots. When the alcohol hit me and things started spinning, all I wanted to do was go home. Immediately. I asked the Bouncer to get me a taxi, and I slipped out of my party. Midway home, I told the Taxi Driver to stop the cab and let me out. I was going to be sick or pass out, I wasn't sure which. Thankfully I came out of my alcohol induced stupor just in time to scream at the Taxi Driver "leave me alone or I will report you" fending him off my partially naked body and stopping him from pulling off more of my clothes.

No matter what I tried, it was always slightly awkward or strange or unusual. I did manage to pull off memorable, every time. I got somewhat comfortable planning my own parties so I would never have to face disappointment, or my fear of not being enough. I always hoped there would be a day where I would give over the pressure and the neurosis and just relax into my one Mel day of the year. I imagined a time where I would do nothing and fall into a delightfully planned celebration where I was patted, stroked, loved and told how terrific I was with no effort being spent on my front. People where supposed to celebrate your light beaming down onto the earth after all. Why was I trying so hard?

Imagine hearing this, "I hate birthdays. I hate holidays. I hate the whole goddamm manufactured bullshit hallmark manipulated marketing force fed holidays," every single time a holiday came around. Can you imagine? Maybe you've been there. I had asked my Man what we could do on my birthday to be met with this vitriolic tirade. I came from the exact opposite place. I enjoy celebrations. Small and wide, I like to acknowledge people, and while I don't need a holiday to remind me how special they are to me; there's no reason not to heap on more affection on an appointed day.

It is interesting I would choose to spend my life with someone who couldn't handle supporting me on my birthday or enjoying any holiday without being angst or anxiety ridden. Interesting that a holiday was always a point of stress and distress.

As my imagined control crumbled, and my marriage was on its last legs, I decided to let my Man plan a birthday celebration for me. After ten years it seemed only fair. Was it a test? Yes. A test to face that which I feared. I would fight through his resistance and see what happened. After much ballyhoo and back and forth, I gave him an idea that would be simple to pull off. He did exactly what I asked him to do. It wasn't perfect. It felt like it does when you force somebody to do something they can't deliver. The day began with me picking up my own birthday cake at the local bakery and ended with me crying myself to sleep.

A year passed and my first "Man free" birthday arrived. I had been through a tough year; things had changed; my perspective was different. I wasn't afraid of no one caring about me, because I was getting a grip on caring about myself, turning that elusive corner on liking myself. I toyed with planning a party, but I didn't know who to invite, what to do, and the new emerging Mel didn't need to carry the birthday torch. It had lost its charge. I would be fine doing nothing. No birthday plans except taking care of myself. As it turned out three of my close friends invited me to a Jazz night at the Hollywood Bowl and let me take the lead on timing and leaving and joining and celebrating at my pace. No pressure. They brought dinner, wine, dessert. It was so pleasant not to have to deal with anything. Not to feel pressured or distressed in any way and to just sit back and soak up the music, the stars and the love of some close friends.

In preparation for this first "Man free" birthday, my therapist gave me a heads up. She let me know that birthdays can mean many different things. Choosing to look at it as a beginning, a re-birth, could be another step in healing. A time to reflect on what had passed, and begin again. Seemed like a great idea.

It's hard for me to admit that I wanted my Man to call, email or extend himself with birthday wishes for me as the day rolled around. One of those, "Hey, things happen, turn out the way they do, but you meant something to me and just wanted you to know. Happy birthday!"

The day passed without a call or an e-mail or a card from my ex Man. After ten years, I was a tiny bit surprised. But why would I have thought anything would have changed? Why would I have thought my wanting it to happen would make it so? I made note of it and tried not to be too disappointed or judgemental. A couple of days after my birthday, I went to my post office box to pick up my mail. Amazingly, there was a #10 envelop from my Ex Man! I felt a moment of satisfaction. After everything we had been through, at least he did send me some type of note for by birthday. Cool.

Not cool.

I opened it up to find the stamped court divorce paperwork from the Judge. The stamp on the court paperwork was August 16th, my birth date. My first thoughts were, what an asshole my ex Man is. Not only did he not remember or choose to wish me a happy birthday on my day, but he would slap me in the face by having the divorce paperwork stamped with my birth date. How could he do that, have this done on my birthday?

Unbelievably not cool.

I took a breath. Wait a minute. My perspective suddenly shifted to reality, a new realization. It wasn't him. Maybe the end was the beginning. Maybe the universe had stepped in to make a statement. My birthday was truly a birth - day. The stamp with my birth date on it at the top of our divorce paperwork gave me closure and gave me a reason to rejoice.

The court stamp to end my marriage and my birthday joined in a universal dance of destiny.

I accepted the stamp with a certain amount of awe and inspiration.

Pride

Pride is definitely the most offending of all of my quirks.

> *Pride cares not who it harms*
> *Pride wears many outfits*
> *Pride takes many forms*
> *Pride demands attention*
> *Pride clouds the truth*
> *Pride tangled with ego and nobody won*

Escape from pride. Escape from ego. It must be possible.

> *I came out alone on my way to my tryst.*
> *But who is this me in the dark?*
> *I move aside to avoid his presence but I escape him not.*
> *He makes the dust rise from the earth with his swagger;*
> *He adds his loud voice to every word I utter.*
> *He is my own little self, my lord, he knows no shame;*
> *But I am ashamed to come to thy door in his company.*

Rab Tagore's poem on ego has always rattled me. Pride and ego. There is no doubt I have been shamed by both. "Pack up your old point of view and I'll promise you a happy ending."

It's a strange feeling to have lived through an altered state and to look back from a different vantage point. I agree very much with Tallulah Bankhead, "if I had my life to live again. I'd make the same mistakes only sooner." I remember all of it. The good and bad.

Blazingly real in all its forms and areas pride drove my determination to make everything right. I was driven to succeed at any cost. No matter that I didn't know what I was trying to succeed at. When I let go, I experienced dying. I went through casting off a few selves on my way to the Bare Mel. Pride was a time, a place and a container that wrapped many of my feelings in its embrace. Making peace with pride fueled my growth. I could use its power and purpose and not get entangled in its pitfalls. I can make this statement. I am clear of my mania. Clear of my judgemental self. Clear of that ever present voice of ego and pride railing against my happiness and soul's purpose. Pride is not a blind mistress but a terrifyingly evil creature determined to bring about our worst.

My pride and my opinion of myself and my ego and worry about what others thought could at last be in balance. Through remembrance and reality and discovery I overcame these demons. I was no longer tortured by these two, and could call them friends. It didn't mean I wouldn't be hurt again, that my pride wouldn't cause me grief. It didn't mean that I would enter some blissful land where nothing got to me. It meant that I could live in equanimity with my two nemeses.

Letting Go

What I didn't know about letting go was that it was going to be a daily, hourly, lifelong quest. Let go. Let go. Let Go. If you love something, for goodness sake set it free.

I would philosophically tell clients during negotiations that you have to be willing to let go to have any chance of getting what you want. If you are afraid to lose you can never engage satisfactorily.

Sometimes it is so easy to give advice about letting go and so hard to follow it. I held on to so many things for fear letting go would destroy me, that I trapped myself in a panic. A panic I couldn't escape from, a panic that frightened me.

In the weeks before the final dissolution date of my marriage, I found myself typing this note to my therapist.

Wow. I'm totally feeling out of my skin. I am grasping around over these weeks. I was exhausted after our chat. I went to an event last night... and when I got home, went to sleep com-

pletely grief stricken and traumatized. I'm going to be free...
free of everything, and I guess I'm scared and nervous.
I made a few promises to myself...

1) No matter what I would push through my fear and
anxiety when support was offered
2) I would finish whatever writing ideas I started without the
fear of acceptance (financial, critical etc.)
3) I would 'be myself' enthusiastically and without regret

Thanks to the work we've done together, one and two
are looking good and three is brightening.

Her response helped me tremendously.

I would expect a lot of grief would be coming up now. Letting
go --- even if it is letting go in a positive way, brings up grief.
In addition, the legal ending of your marriage, even if it feels
like a relief, would probably bring up grief as you let go. Keep
breathing through it and ride the fluctuating pain with as little
resistance as possible.

"Ride the pain with as little resistance as possible." Let
go. Know that grief is part of the process. It is so helpful to see
something you need to hear in writing.

> *The moving finger writes; and having writ,*
> *moves on: nor all thy piety nor wit*
> *Shall lure it back to cancel half a line,*
> *Nor all thy tears wash out a word of it.*
> *Omar Khayyam*

Recovery to me was so about mastering letting go, well, actually being able to let go, understanding its nuances and its powers and then moving on.

Once you let go, you made a choice. Don't bemoan or spend energy feeding what comes up; notice that it is tough, feel it, embrace it, but let it pass. Do not let it drag you down.

I would never have thought the ten minutes through the corn fields to get milk and eggs from the local dairy farm growing up would be replaced by a trip down Rodeo Drive in Beverly Hills to the Whole Foods Market. I would never have thought so many things were possible if I hadn't taken a first step and let go of what I had known.

There is no way I could have drawn a map that would have led me to where I am.

Some of the difficulty and my personal angst would come from trying to achieve results in a ball busting straightforward linear fashion. When I let go of that which confined me or defined me I ended up where I wanted to be. Without fail.

I learned to love letting go.

Redemption

Everything about redemption is near and dear to my heart. I get weepy over second chances. I love when someone takes responsibility, reclaims themselves, and is forgiven. I cry and am moved by the ability of the human race to forgive. Something about redemption's code, overcoming insurmountable odds, rising from the ashes and being accepted gets me every time.

A favorite real estate agent friend of mine, having seen it all, resigned every dilemma or discussion or choice to the inevitable "no worries." Afraid to make the commitment to buy a home with him, "Buy it, you can always sell." Afraid to marry him because there are a few quirks in his personality, you can always get a divorce." "Afraid to have kids with him, when you break up, you'll have a built in baby sitter." Everything had a resilient, "not to worry." I looked up to her philosophy; you can always make a change, a choice and move to a new understanding, a new perspective. Nothing wrong with making the choice. Don't be afraid. Get it done. You will always come out on the other side. Redemption from perceived disaster always possible. The funny part, it is perceived, not reality. You are imagining it will be tough, tiring, troublesome etc. You don't know. Why worry about something now?

Last year - Breakup

This year - Divorce

Next year - Who knows

Every moment represents the choice to be different, to stand up to what you are afraid of, to go in a different direction no matter how set, how stuck. Every breath can represent something new.

This breath can represent a change.

This breath a new direction.

This breath the reclaiming of some dream.

This breath redeeming hope.

Resigned can be a thing of the past. Heartache doesn't disappear but is replaced slowly, quickly, hard to say. Change travels its own course. Allow yourself to enjoy the process even though it feels different. It is scary; it is tough; notice it and do it anyway.

I wake up and fight every day. I fight for a new tomorrow. I fight for the chance to make a difference. I fight for the opportunity to have the life that I want. I fight for all those who will come behind me, and I fight to beat my own drum however terrible or special it might sound.

Redemption knows its time and it knows its place.

It awaits the call.

Always

Weird that there was a time when looking at myself as a complete and utter failure was the way to start the day. To think that I would never be able to succeed at anything. That I would never be good enough.

What a tremendous distortion of the truth.

My goal for this change year was to be a better me. It didn't seem possible when the words rolled from my tongue at the beginning of last year. My self loathing was at an all time high. It didn't matter that it would be a battle, it didn't matter that I had no idea what I was doing or how I could make it happen. The important thing was setting the goal to be "a better me" and taking that first step.

The most important thing I learned was the body knows and has healing powers beyond anything we can realize or understand. It will aid in its own healing. Its own recovery. Maybe not in the time you want it to, but it will reveal itself if given the proper time and attention. The brain owns a powerful place in the body. The mind and body connection - intricate and incredible. Knowing the magnitude and power of bringing these two pieces together in harmony fills me with hope that I can meet any challenge to come.

You reach a point where tears are friends beckoning a truth you had locked away in a drawer.

> *A bird finds its own perch*
> *Glowing in the warmth*
> *Reaching for the next bend*
> *Going beyond the rock*
> *Walking that extra distance*
> *Seeing what's ahead.*

Incredible.

I found I could be so much more. I could allow myself to enjoy support even though it was scary. I could go beyond any barrier I had set for myself. I could live in the knowledge that my truth was enough. That I am enough and I always was.

Breakthrough

A moment came where despair was too much to carry. I thought and fought and tried and cried and came to a realization one quiet afternoon on a drive in Los Angeles traffic. I was fighting the wrong battle. I was never going to make everyone okay; not only that, it would be an impossible task for anyone. I had nothing to prove to be a member of the human race.

What a relief. How simple. How pure. How true.

I eased into myself as never before.

There are many recipes for despair. I can only give you mine. Constantly explaining myself, never feeling good enough, being unable to ask for what I wanted without second guessing myself, trying to make everyone feel better, trying to take care of everyone else's feelings. Stir that up, pop it in the oven, and it is a potent combination for despair and distress. I wish I could say the divorce was a main ingredient to the recipe, but it wasn't the case. It just added its own icing or topping. I had long ago entered the field of despair. Pleasing others and never feeling I was in my own skin, it was only a matter of time before I was debilitated.

It is interesting how far you'll go to create and embellish a recipe that isn't working to try to make it work. Adjusted behavior, changed ideals, individualized efforts all grasping for acceptance. It was a constant battle. In concert with interactions with others, this recipe became deadly. My empathy a weight, instead of the gift that it was.

The day I burned my recipe - I changed my vantage point to acceptance. I became a Mel-o-maniac. I started to accept, then I started to root, then I started to cheer, then I started to celebrate.

I am flawed, special, different, not cool, klutzy, tenacious, understanding, empathetic, curious, creative and emotional. I celebrate all of it. I allow myself to enjoy all these imperfect things that make me perfect. I told myself over and over again I was worthy to be part of this species of humanity that I loved so dearly. I kept repeating. I'm not different. I am enough. I was at once here and together with all the souls and spaces of the world. I relied on past teachers, poets, the arts; I found solace and opened up the floodgates of acceptance.

What a tremendous gift I gave myself, this joyous integration of all that life has to offer with all that I am. I thank despair. I embrace despair. I celebrate despair. Because despair brought me realizations, understandings, letting gos and most importantly freedom. Free to frolic into the wondrous and unknown future.

"All the curses have been ended, the reverses wiped away."

The possibility of being found, which holds beauty and terror. The possibility of becoming. I started to soak up ideas. I started to know that the first steps always need to be taken to get to any destination and to take those first steps I never had to be all knowing or to put it mildly, good.

You cannot get there from here if you think you have to be good. And that's the truth. Kander and Ebb sum it up...

> *Just when it seems we're out of dreams,*
> *and things have got us down.*
> *We don't despair, we don't go there,*
> *we hang our bonnets out of town.*
> *So there's no doubt we're well cut out*
> *We just run life's marathon, we just move on,*
> *we just move on.*

The caps are off, the sprinkler system and the stream is flowing freely, pumping and pulsing and shouting and spouting with nothing to contain it, restrain it. In the flow, in the throw, a pulsing energy saying possibilities.

It is so easy to focus on things that hurt us. The evil pain, the desperate despair. It squawks so loudly. But if you tune yourself in to listen to other, softer voices, you can set yourself up for eye opening good times, you can make the choice to find the flower that drifts from a tree and lands on your windshield, to notice the butterfly that holds itself in the wind on its way to freedom. To feel the perfect crunch of grass on a dew filled morning. To bend down to pick up that unique fall leaf that bursts with its own individuality. Pain and despair and turmoil and laughs and joy and exhilaration live side by side and coexist at glorious times across our timelines. Get comfortable with all; know they are meant to speak to you, that everything is a gift, and you are stepping toward freedom by seeing across a wider canvas.

White Orchids

I knew I had crossed a threshold as I found myself re-reading these words. "Who would have thought having someone stand with me in the confusion and continually provide a voice of, reason, truth, love, support, you name it, would help me find my own. And then once finding it and helping me listen to it would also help me figure out how to use it."

When asked if love ever rebounded to embrace the past I had to say yes. When I chose to grant myself freedom. When I chose to live in letting go. The world could work on my behalf. The past could be part of my future. Freedom was about accepting help. Freedom was living my life. My way.

As the many issues I dealt with paraded in front of me, as I faced all the failed relationships, as I experienced what everyone had to teach me... it was a lot. Whenever I felt like it was too much, I had my 'Go To' Team. I wasn't alone. And I knew I could make it. I could get through whatever happened.

My team was anchored by my Therapist and my Life Coach. These two anchors helped me go deeper and higher than I could have ever gone on my own.

George Balanchine, regarded as the "Father of American Ballet," had a belief while pushing limits and getting bigger, more extraordinary results from his dancers that everyone learns a certain amount and thinks, "Enough, finally I'm done;" I've arrived. When pushed, they are surprised to discover, "Wow, I can do that!?" In response to the person's surprise at their own results, Balanchine always said, "Yes, you can."

People see what they want to see. Seeds became an image that kept coming into my consciousness. My Therapist talked of being given a gift of wild white orchids, which she planted on the side of her house and completely forgot about. A year later she turned the corner on the side of her house and to her surprise was greeted with blossoming abundant white orchids, flowering and flourishing beautifully.

I had many conversations about the soul's code, watermelon seeds never became sunflowers, acorns never became pine trees. Images of seeds came to me all the time, these many images centered on creating the right environments to let whatever was imprinted emerge.

There are critical passages and altering events you experience along the path. All of them represent opportunities that have always been there but you hadn't the eyes to see for whatever reason.

Having help gives you extra sets of eyes, extra acumen, extra insights. There's no end to the value of objective observations and evaluations of your perspectives.

When I first started with my Therapist it was a couple's appointment. After a few sessions it was clear I needed individual help. Lots of help. Initially I made the link to something I always wanted. A mentor. Over our time together she occupied varied roles, all of them helpful.

Many turning points came and went. Blow outs occurred. Getting through was always on the agenda, and she was with me through everything. She carried the ball on the breakup. She guided my emotional development. She taught me what a nourishing relationship means. Free from the need for approval and reciprocation. She took away two of my overdeveloped Mel muscles, listening and helping. Until our work together, these were the only ways I knew how to interact with anyone. By forcing me to speak into the clear air and accept help, I grew new muscles and enhanced my abilities to connect to people in different ways.

There were points where I got scared of my feelings of attachment, neediness, where all the support and help became overwhelming. I would freak out, and have anxiety for days. I knew it was just a false alarm. That the alarm was telling me I needed to experiment with living in the land of being overwhelmed with this fullness of life, experience and emotions. To do whatever was necessary to let it be. To move past my anxiety. That just because I was comfortable being uncomfortable didn't make it right.

It took a long time to crack the protective wall between me and everyone else. The wall was now gone. Destroyed. No going back. I felt completely exposed. Not the kind of exposed where you are caught naked and a couple of people saw a bit more than they needed to. This was full and complete body and soul exposure.

When it happened I spent an entire session motor mouthing trying to speak and not be heard. Trying not to feel anything. I was too afraid. Without the wall I was grasping to cover myself with a fog of anxiety and sound. I couldn't bring myself to hear anything. Either way. Right or wrong. Because it would, I thought, swamp me in too much love and understanding and put me completely out of existence. As I literally sweated through the hour, babbling away, I felt feverish and humiliated when I left. I knew I had to face the music, that our next session needed to involve me embracing my emotions. The intimacy I had been afraid of for so long.

I couldn't have been more terrified.

Every part of me was flooded. My anxiety raged. I was scared and looking for assurance. This time I knew where to turn. My Life Coach, my best girl, my friend of many years. Like Sherlock Holmes piecing together an anxiety puzzle, she clicked me into the solid color of the Rubik's cube that I had been working so hard to solve. She helped me make the connections. Clearly and simply and beautifully. It was definitely akin to the satisfying release of tension you have on the final pages of a delicious murder mystery thriller... "That's who did it and how."

Knowledge of the connections brought me peace.

I could now face thinking about bringing this particular and quirky breakup journey to a conclusion. I was no longer the confused person that had picked up the phone to get some answers all those months ago. It reminded me of that

Zen proverb, before enlightenment, chopping wood, carrying water. After enlightenment, chopping wood, carrying water. Everything had changed but I was still me doing what I do.

Saying goodbye, was a place and time I didn't want to face. I didn't know how to navigate evolving the few important relationships I had. Moving them to a new place. Discovering deeper levels free from my fear. No matter how tough. No matter how much anxiety reared its head when I contemplated goodbye. I had to let go. It had been a powerful, transformative experience. My old identity would be missed. But my new identity, which was now large enough to hold so much more, was deafeningly calling my name. The anxiety over the loss of my old identity, I told myself, was normal. I clearly saw it was just the past trying one final time to get me to stay in its deformed clutches. Knowing this, I sat and wrote with my anxiety hand in hand. I worked with it side by side. I explained and explained to myself why I felt the way I did. Why anxiety was gripping me like a python. I kept moving through. I couldn't stop it. So I let it be.

As I finished my anxiety-filled writings and thoughts, I needed a cheese steak. Badly. Coming from the East Coast there are certain cries of the wild, certain must haves in the lands. One of them was a Philly-like cheese steak. Hot dogs qualify; Dunkin' Donuts when pressed; Tasty Kakes when feeling blue. There are a thousand things that fall in the East Coast comfort food category, and I welcomed my needs for them. When they called, I tried to answer.

Beverly Hills happens to have a pretty good version of the cheese steak shop in the form of Papa Jake's Subs. I had never

been there, but my brother's recommendation had been ringing in my ears for months and months. When I pushed out
of Papa Jake's doors with a luscious 12" cheese steak under
my arm into a gorgeous sunny day, I saw it. The Beverly Hills
Seed Company -- since 1927. As I approached the beautiful
picture windows, I could see it was completely filled top to
bottom with white orchids.

I knew looking at the lovely shop filled with orchids, I
was in the flow of life. I was in conversation with the world.
Seeds had been born and could grow. The thread of the eternal
was an undercurrent to everything that was going on.

Unwillingly and unknowingly I had found the convic-
tion to face some final hurdles. The stage had been set without knowing how the clues would play themselves out. The
guideposts had been outlined. The journey toward self didn't
need to be a solo performance and would open up the universe at my feet.

I could move on with help from those that offered, free
from the fear that help would destroy me.

The courage had been drawn from the love and support
volunteered, and the steps had evolved into something magical and mysterious. Like inspired colors slashing across a canvas with seemingly random abandon, the brush strokes filled
in, revealing everything.

As I stood there awash in all the exposed feelings that
had been bottled up, all the moments and emotions that had
been squashed, as I released the bitter recriminations that
held me captive, I felt a tingle of an almost orgasmic release
flood through my body. Something bigger than I pushed me
forward and beyond. Alignment and expulsion of the black

hole of knowledge exploding into the future of all that would be. Like a mountain climber using a buddy system complete with levers and pulleys so missteps wouldn't result in premature death, the mountain that needed to be toppled was conquered.

Saying goodbye was no longer painful and traumatic. Because, it wasn't goodbye, it was good times. My team and process would always be there. My team would always be with me. When the growing got tough, I could lean on them. We had been through it all. We travelled together through laughs, warmth, fear, frolic, neurosis, anxieties, love, trust, trauma and it was all okay.

What can you say about people that helped you through some of the most challenging passages on the human development map? Who stood with you, who counseled and provided services, who anchored some incredibly stormy patches. "Hey thanks, you saved my life, my marriage, myself, my tuna fish sandwich, whatever." No matter how I looked at it, nothing did it justice. It's more like "You've helped me live my life. You share a special place in all that follows." Transformation and trust. Triumph and tenacity. Guidance and giving. There's a balance in a success that is shared.

In the end I had no choice to do what I did. The choice to face my fears of being alone, of not being enough, of not being good, of not making sense, of needing help, had to be met. I had reached a point where I felt safe and it was okay and I knew it was time to move that safety forward. That feeling safe for the first time wasn't the ending but only a beginning. And in that choice of choosing help I gave myself a power. The power to choose. The power to make choices for me.

Alive

For so long, I looked and looked and wondered, never thinking I could reach the end. It was like some long forgotten fog that never cleared. Always there, heavy and lingering. Always feeling and dragging and clinging.

"Notice every tree, recognize the light. I want to know how to get through, through to something new. Something of my own" again from Sunday in the Park with George.

Linking my own self worth to other people's ideas coming to fruition was a folly. A horrific habit that I battled to retrain. A battle that will be an ongoing part of who I am.

Coming alive was a gradual process, a not so strong jolt of continual understanding that would beat against the fog. With each beat things got clearer and clearer. I was not meant to be standing strongly alone crossing the finish line like some Olympic athlete on the final run of the decathlon. Victories came in small and large doses over time. This beat of truth gently brought me into focus. The fantasies that surrounded me and diminished me began to disappear, replaced with a knowing that there are individuals and there are groups. There are mistakes, there are accidents, there are friends and there are enemies, there are people who wish you well and people who wish you ill, and that's all cool. We are all interdependent on each other. I could disagree with others and still be me. I could need someone and still be me. I could be hurt and still be me. Like some long lost stranger, I was coming home. Home to everything that was forgotten but familiar. Home to a place where I could be. I was on my own, but still I knew I wasn't alone.

> *Sometimes people leave you*
> *Others may deceive you*
> *You decide what's right*
> *You decide what's good*
> *You decide alone*
> *But no one is alone.*

How wonderful to know what it means to be alive. Sondheim had it right, you decide. To awake into the light or darkness to feel whole and be at peace knowing at any moment something amazing can happen. You just need to open the doors and breathe.

"Live and love as hard as you know how. Make this moment last because the best of times is now." Jerry Herman La Cage Aux Folles

There isn't a part of me that hasn't come alive.

The Bare Melcessities

Finding my voice was harder than I would have ever realized. Years of falseness needed to come down. So many levels and crusts and upheavals protecting what? Me? Please. I loved every moment of trying to get bare. I loved the confusion, the struggles, the getting down to the essentials. The starts and stops, the tears and sorrow and the unbending belief in something greater than myself, something invisible, something magical.

Why do we work so hard to get what we don't want? And how do we get turned around to chasing something that was there all along? It had been a long time of not addressing what I wanted, what was important to me. The idea of propping others up so I'd be okay never occurred to me as a problem. Just helpful. Altruistic.

The beginnings of a new Mel were laughable. Coltish became my favorite description. I had many things to learn, many experiments to try, and always the practice, practice, and more practice. I'm still self absorbed could have been my refrain through much of this overhaul. Everything consumed so the world could open up again.

I had to learn who was "safe" to experiment with in this formative stage. The practice became the perfection and the practice keeps me on track.

I still laugh about finding my voice and still having to practice articulating what I wanted and owning what I meant. Speaking up for myself had been so terrifying, so anxiety producing, I had to work at it. Each failure a success, practice moved me forward and those failed successes became second nature in the journey of staying in my element. Failure just part of the fun. Something to be embraced.

After so many years going one way, there is a tremendous amount of joy and discovery and triumph in allowing yourself to embrace a new direction. I was "tough" enough for such a long time. Until I cracked. It took a lot of effort to redirect the action and energy, to know how to deal with it, express it, work with it, change it. Amazingly, I learned how.

I knew a strength that can only come from facing some hard truths. From seeing a mountain seemingly too high to climb and taking the steps to climb it anyway. The coolest part, reaching the top wasn't the satisfaction point, it was living on the other side, making mistakes, and growing in the sunlight and sunset of that new day, living with the scars forever a part of who I was, with no fear of others seeing those scars. I had accepted the whole picture, no longer caught in recriminations and distress over some imagined picture of perfection that could never be achieved. Everything contributed to the person that I was. The total picture. Me. At last.

> *I'd love for you to know me well*
> *To see me falling into place*
> *To see the face behind the face behind the face*
> *I'd love for you to see me clear*
> *With all my virtues and my lies*
> *With all the pleasure and pain around the eyes*

I can't tell you how many times I played Edward Kleban's terrific Self Portrait from A Class Act over this year of change.

> *I want the opportunity to show you*
> *The whole damn display*
> *To open like a flower*
> *And to know you will stay*
> *I wish that you would take me home*
> *And take the time to work me out*
> *To say there she is, that's what she's about*
> *The joy of her, the silliness, the hell*
> *I'd love for you to know me very well.*

When outer success no longer distracts from a deeper knowing, the Bare Melcessities will come to you.

In the same way the notion of the end rises in our consciousness, the notion of something beautiful sings its way into being. To stand in that being makes me stronger than I ever thought I could be. It feeds me. I am contented. I feel like dancing. Positively ready to do kick lines with the Rockettes. Be prepared if you see me. Look out. How do you keep that feeling going? Ah. The question. The question that unravels all questions. You don't. You accept the whole picture, the ups, the downs, the joys, the awkward, the awful, the ecstasy, as Lerner and Lowe put it at the end of My Fair Lady "All second nature to me now, like breathing out and breathing in." I've chosen to accept it all as a happenstance of occurrence. A grand tour of all that life can be, filled with what's important, the simple Bare Melcessities.

How does the story end? It doesn't. It continues.

It all awaits.

Epilogue

The process of getting to the Bare Melcessities has been richly rewarding and deeply satisfying. I allowed myself to enjoy all of it. I didn't push (too much). I didn't try to do anything more than experience 'Old Mother Nature's' recipes. I sat and felt and typed. Thank you for going with me in my new direction and helping me learn.

I had started the year with the goal to become a better me. As the year passes by, I stride into a new goal of becoming the best me I can be.

It was a great exercise to pick some topics and share. I learned so much through my turmoil. I learned how I want to be in the world. I learned how to find meaning and security by facing problems on my own, and I learned not to be afraid of asking for help. I learned to allow myself to enjoy support, even though it was scary. I learned how to accept my tears as a part of the whole. The whole that includes the dark and the light, the laughter and the derision. I learned how to be the tree and not worry that I wasn't the squirrel.

It is just so cool to have been able to type out these ideas and feel secure that while everyone might not relate, I won't be thrown out of the human race for not succeeding. Little Mel finally able to tell some truths and be fine with it. "No more curses you can't undo."

Now if I say something I mean it. If I feel something, I share it and if I want something, you know it. I can't tell you how much easier it is. So less complicated.

I am brought to nourishing remembrances of the consider-
ations that have been afforded me through this time of change.
Beauty and ugliness danced around me; demons battled over
my peace of mind, and I came out the other side. I remember
reading Fluer Adcock's poem Weathering reflecting on a year
spent away and coming to a long fought acceptance of the
perfection that already is within us in the midst of my chaos
and I knew, the magnificence of self acceptance was a choice,
a choice I had made for me.

> *My face catches the wind*
> *from the snow line*
> *and flushes with a flush*
> *that will never wholly settle.*
> *Well, that was a metropolitan vanity,*
> *wanting to look young forever, to pass.*
> *I was never a pre-Raphaelite beauty*
> *and only pretty enough to be seen*
> *with a man who wanted to be seen*
> *with a passable woman.*
> *But now that I am in love*
> *with a place that doesn't care*
> *how I look and if I am happy,*
> *happy is how I look and that's all.*
> *My hair will grow grey in any case,*
> *my nails chip and flake,*
> *my waist thicken, and the years*
> *work all their usual changes.*

If my face is to be weather beaten as well,

it's little enough lost

for a year among the lakes and vales

where simply to look out my window

at the high pass

makes me indifferent to mirrors

and to what my soul may wear

over its new complexion.

Take a walk around the lake and look for the Bare Melcessities. The simple Bare Melcessities.

Andiamo!

ACKNOWLEDGEMENTS

I am deeply grateful to all the people who opened their doors, opened their homes, and opened their hearts.

Thank you Gena Kay and Gina Rugolo. Thank you to tough talking legal eagle Howard Alperin. Thank you to my dear friends Roger Harrison, Jonna Tamases and Craig Marshall for living lives that inspire. Thanks to my Brothers, Brian and Chris, for the emotional support and laugh filled dinners. Thanks to the Gribbon family. Thanks to Greg and Nola Talmage for the home cooked meals and the nurturing love and concern. Thanks to big Viv and little Viv. Thanks to my parents for always being there. Thank you Bill Miltenberger. Thank you Ellen Dux and Paul Madeira. Thanks to my soulful sister friends Michelle Archer, Sue Bailey, Joy Di Palma, Sheri Levy, Julie Magbojos, Kathleen McMahon, Kearie Peak, Shane Selleck, and Ms. Sally Vail. Thanks to Dr. Bosten for the laughs through the pain. Thank you Jake, Josie and Jasper. Thank you Moses Brown, Oliver, Minnie, Blake O'Malley and Maggie. Thank you Santiago Herrera, Jr. for creating the books interior. Thanks to the enchanted streets of Reevesbury and Westwanda and all who join me on my nightly walks.

Thanks to that source I can't name and can't explain for sending me on this path. A path I continue to walk. Humbled and nourished by all I encounter.

And lastly. To Frank... you will be missed.

ABOUT THE AUTHOR

MELANIE LUTZ is a writer
living in Los Angeles, California.
For more information, visit her website
www.melanielutz.com.

LaVergne, TN USA
24 September 2009
158869LV00001B/54/P